D1487467

HELP—A Guide to Counseling and Therapy without a Hassle

This book will tell you, the modern-day teen, who offers professional help and how, and what it can and can't accomplish. Today there is a great deal of creative, hassle-free help available for those who are resourceful enough to seek it out and sane enough to use it. Here is everything you want to know about therapy and counseling. Fears and myths are eliminated as the author tells how natural it is to want to talk to someone about bothersome problems; why sometimes friends and family are *not* the people to confide in; how it takes not a weak person, but a strong, self-determined individual to realize professional help is desirable.

In addition to explaining the work of and differences among psychiatrists and psychologists, counseling clergymen, social workers, counselors, and so on, the author explains how you can choose a competent therapist yourself; who can help you other than a therapist or counselor; and the pluses and minuses of individual and group therapy. Since parents play a major role in your life, the book gives you hints on how to deal with your parents—not only how to get them to accept the fact that you want help, but even how to get *them* involved in the therapy process with you.

HELP shows you how to size up your progress; how to determine how well therapy worked for you; and how to tell when you're "done."

But this chatty, informal, information-loaded look at your emotions and hang-ups and what you can do about them does even more than all of the above. It tells you that by seeking help you are finally getting in touch with yourself, setting out to take charge of your own life.

H E L P

A Guide to Counseling and Therapy without a Hassle

Jane Marks

JULIAN MESSNER
NEW YORK

Published by Julian Messner, a Simon & Schuster Division of
Gulf & Western Corporation. Simon & Schuster Building,
1230 Avenue of the Americas, New York, N.Y. 10020.
All rights reserved.

Second Printing, 1977

/ 0 9 5 7~

Library of Congress Cataloging in Publication Data

Marks, Jane.
    HELP: a guide to counseling and therapy without a hassle.

    Bibliography: p. 185.
    Includes index.
    SUMMARY: Advice for the teen-ager on choosing professional
help, what it can accomplish, the pluses and minuses of individual and group therapy, how to deal with parents, and how
to determine one's progress.
    1. Adolescent   psychiatry—Juvenile   literature.   2. Psycho-
therapy—Juvenile literature.   3. Counseling—Juvenile literature.
4. Consumer education—Juvenile literature. [1. Psychotherapy.
2. Psychology.   3. Counseling]   I. Title.
RJ503.M29   616.8'914   76-23375
ISBN 0-671-32811-5 (lib. bdg.)

Printed in the United States of America

for Bob and Joshua

Acknowledgments

For permission to excerpt and reprint material in this book, the author and publisher are grateful to the following:

Office of Youth Development
for excerpt from "Boston's Bridge: A Streetwork Program that Builds Trust with Clients." Published in *Youth Reporter*, OHD/OYD 75-26030. April, 1975.

Contents

Introduction

" Please, Sigmund, I'd rather do it myself."

Anyone with a grain of sensitivity should be able to figure out what's bothering him, right? Who wants some outsider poking in? It's great to be introspective—and to be good at it—but it is notoriously inefficient all by itself. When there isn't any established structure or outside person to keep you working at it, and when results are slow in coming, there's a temptation to quit. It's hard enough to stick with a simple New Year's resolution or a morning exercise routine.

Even if you are willing to sustain the effort, "self-shrinkage" still doesn't do much. You can keep a journal of your moods and feelings, and come up with insights that are very accurate and discerning, but in order to convert that self-knowledge from the journal pages back to real life, most people need a skilled and sympathetic human listener.

According to the book

You must have seen them: dozens of books which purport to offer a special recipe or crash course for getting into your head, finding peace, and discarding every trace of a hang-up. All you have to do is walk into a bookstore or library and you'll find a proliferation of the latest books on a variety of new and slightly used self-therapy schemes—each one billing itself as *the* important breakthrough.

Anyone can study those books—or go to special open-to-the-public lectures and workshops—until the cows come home, but they are not likely to become particularly adept at fixing up their own situations, because too often that "neat" formula serves only to disguise a continuing problem.

Haven't you known someone like Bess, the girl with an obesity problem? Hating the fact that she weighed a hefty 200 pounds, Bess read everything she could find on dieting and the psychology of overeating, and she even discussed her problem at length with the librarian, the counterman at the luncheonette she stopped into frequently, and anyone else who was polite enough to listen. After a while, however, Bess discovered that with all her assiduous attention to her problem, she had fallen behind in her courses and gained an extra 30 pounds.

There are people who claim that self-help is the only acceptable help because they are so "independent." They say this in such a way as to suggest that it is only the immature and the gutless who "scurry" off to see a therapist. Actually, it is the so-called rugged individualist who is scared: scared, for instance, that if he lets down his guard he will be swept away in a flood of messy feelings he would just as soon avoid. What he doesn't realize is that in therapy he could work on that fear and perhaps discover that needing someone else is normal and fine and won't undermine the whole identity struggle. (In fact, the net result could be a more relaxed and easier relationship with the people around— and a better feeling about oneself.)

Therapy begins at home—or does it?

Many people think of therapy as a last resort—for people with no friends or family. Why else, they wonder, would anyone pay money to a total stranger when all kinds of loving and familiar people are available to help?

Well, it's great to be surrounded by love and concern; in fact, it's fantastic. We all know that. So it's a reasonable question: aren't close people better than any hired helper? For some personal problems, the answer is yes; but there is a point at which amateur help—no matter how enthusiastic—is simply not enough.

First, helping someone takes more patience and more skill than most people can muster without a lot of training. Listening—and talking—may seem like things that anyone can do, but just because therapy doesn't involve special tools like scalpels or acupuncture needles doesn't mean that it isn't a delicate process. It takes subtlety and discipline and some experience to do it well. When you start peeling back the wall of words around a person, the underside is very sensitive and very, very vulnerable.

Distance is another thing. A therapist doesn't have to be a total stranger, but it's best all the way around if the person is sufficiently removed from the center of your universe so that he or she can be objective about you and your feelings. It makes it *much* easier for you to be totally frank with the therapist because you don't have to worry about being tactful.

It takes a devoted friend, a wise parent to realize that they may not be the best ones to help you work out a problem—at least not in every case. Here are some of the misfirings and backfirings that so often happen when you look for help too close to home.

Parents

It may seem like the most logical choice in the world; after all, haven't Mother and Father been helping you in one way or another all your life? They certainly care what happens to you—they probably worry about that more than you do! And they know you right down to the kinds of detailed recollections of your childhood that would boggle a trivia-buff. Chances are, you regarded your parents at one time or another as the wisest and most trustworthy mentors that you could ever hope to find.

Even now, there are some times when a parent can help an awful lot. When Barbara's father was dying of cancer, it meant a great deal to Barbara to be able to share her feelings and fears with her mother.

You're lucky if you have a parent or two who can help you sort out emotional problems, but don't feel cheated if you haven't. All the reasons for why parents "should" be ideal for this kind of aid can backfire and make them absolutely terrible.

First of all, your parents know you far too well to be objective—objective about you and about whatever drummer you're marching to that may be different from theirs. Their involvement—and large role—in your life (even at your age) make them too intense and anxious to merely sit there and listen without getting horrified, making a speech, or trying to save you from yourself. Having so recently served as your keepers and trainers, they tend to be uncomfortable in as well as unsuitable for the task. If they aren't too directive and advice-y or more punitive than helpful in hearing about your problems, they might bend over backwards and be too buddy-buddy: hurling themselves headlong over the generation gap in their overeagerness for your approval.

Most parents love their kids, so give them a break. Don't ask the old folks to take on a role which is so delicate, so difficult, and so truly foreign to being the parent of a young adult.

Caution: Advice may be hazardous
to your friendship

Friends are surely the best people in the world—which is why they might seem like a good source of help for emotional problems. But that can often impose too heavy a burden on both of you!

The relief that comes from spewing out a problem is too often followed by a guilty feeling of having overstepped (despite hasty assurance to the contrary); or you might feel some regret for having been, well . . . less than discreet in baring your soul, leaving yourself so naked. The person you've confided in now knows more about you than you really would like him to know. Will he lord it over you the next time you have a fight? Does he think less of you? Does he really understand? And will he keep it to himself?

There are many reasons why impulsive, unedited outpourings of inner chaos—even into the most receptive and friendliest of ears—not only may not help you, but can loosen the glue on a close and valued friendship.

You may know someone like Stephanie, a girl who relies on her friends for help in analyzing each dramatic new development, each nuance and detail of her sex life (which seems, from her reporting of it, to bring Stephanie more anxiety than pleasure). Anyway, it's not that Stephanie is deliberately showing off or flaunting her behavior; nor is she just seeking an easy confessional. Stephanie is sincerely trying to grapple with her feelings about why she went to bed with so-and-so when she wasn't all that attracted to him, but how the way he looked at her gave her this peculiar sensation down to her toes and why do you suppose that was. . . .

Her well-meaning and caring friends *want* to help. They recognize her distress, but at the same time, they find themselves saying, "Hmmm," looking away, fidgeting, and tuning out. They may be thinking, "Hey, quit forcing me to imagine you doing all those things, stop dragging me into all those intimate scenes of yours."

There are two kinds of pitfalls that the good-friend-deputized-as-shrinker tends to fall into. First, there's the YES-MAN syndrome: the friend telling you what he or she thinks you want to hear. We're not even talking about the pseudo-friend who'll do that simply because it's less taxing than arguing or even thinking about your problem; nor do we mean the so-called friend who is too anxious to be liked to risk annoying you with what he really thinks. We mean the friend who'll say something soothing— sometimes in shocking disregard for the obvious— not for any ulterior motive, but just because he or she really cares for you. ("Oh, you're not too fat, old buddy; 250 pounds is right for your height. You have heavy bones, that's all . . ." or "*Sure* Sam loves you. He'll probably ask you out real soon. I'll bet he's been going with Patty all this time just to make you jealous.") You are very lucky if you have a friend who cares so much for your feelings; it would be a shame to jeopardize a genuine friendship by trying to squeeze ersatz therapy out of it!

The other major pitfall in friends-counseling-friends is the I'LL TELL YOU WHAT TO DO syndrome. The self-appointed architect of your destiny will cheerfully tell you exactly what's wrong with you—at the drop of a mere sigh—and he'll throw in a blueprint of "what you really must do to start living." That's what it was like when Lena, at 17, asked her friend Susan if she should elope with George. Said Sue, "Oh, listen, how can you even dream of tying yourself down to anyone at this age, let alone to someone as far beneath you as dopey George is." (Incidentally, Lena *did* marry George— and never got over hating poor Sue, who hadn't meant to be nasty but was only trying to help Lena the only way she knew how.)

Vested interest

Another obstacle to seeking psychological help from friends is the very fact of their involvement in your life (and you in theirs). Like Carolyn, who is *not* going to feel so very objective about her steady boyfriend John's problems if he tells her that he can't figure out why he keeps having sexy dreams about Carolyn's sister. Or, perhaps, that he feels confused, doubtful, and unloving towards the whole world (Carolyn included). Sure, his feelings are legitimate and worth exploring, but not with Carolyn.

Sometimes people use the form of friends-helping-friends to serve and feed (rather than solve) neurotic inner needs. Take Angie, for example. She lives in Chicago and has just met Warren, a young ex-convict. Warren is recently off drugs, just out of jail (two weeks), and more than a little apprehensive about his future (at this point, his immediate future). Angie has taken him under her wing as combination friend, boyfriend, and dependent little lamb. Warren needs to find *himself* as well as a job. He needs confidence and a sense that he can master the everyday world. Angie, on the other hand, thinks she is helping Warren, but she is really motivated much more compellingly by the need to feel indispensable.

Deep down inside, she's afraid that nobody, including Warren, would stick with her unless they were thoroughly dependent on her. So, while she and Warren play out the charade that she has his best interests at heart and is trying to help him build up his confidence, she's actually allowing—and encouraging—him to become addicted to her "help."

Sometimes it's the other way around—where it's the helpee rather than the helper who's doing the exploiting. "You call yourself my friend, don't you?" Andy says in what could almost be an accusing tone. "Oh," he'll say, wringing his hands to show how much he is suffering, "I guess I've said some rotten things about you—broken confidences and even some lies. Hell, I feel so . . . so *tortured*. I can't even sleep at night . . . maybe I was trying to hurt you because I was jealous of all your success with women. Could that be the source of my conflict? What do you think my root problem is? You are such a strong and patient adult person, I really need you to help me straighten out."

Andy's confession can certainly be considered a cry for help (and he could use some). At this point, though, it would seem that he's not really searching for insight so much as insisting on unconditional acceptance. Friendship was never designed to accommodate such heavy baggage.

That kind of acceptance *can* be found, on the other hand, with a professional helper; in fact, a therapist *encourages* the client to tell all—no matter how deep and dark the secrets may be, no matter how provocative. Far from thinking any the less of you, resenting you, or feeling threatened by what you have to say, a therapist is trained to recognize the psychological underpinnings and to help you see what's really going on in your head. In other words, instead of the emotional reaction, the value judgment, or the dutiful pat that you might get from a friend, a therapist can help you to examine, to discover the person you are. It is much more useful and lasting, more reliable; and you haven't lost a friend in the process.

Anyway, it's something to think about.

1

Needing help/ getting help

We all know how it feels: having personal problems and hurting; trying to cope but not getting very far.

You may have tried talking to your parents or to a friend—or to a succession of them—but it hasn't gotten you anywhere. Perhaps you've bought a book promising a whole new foolproof, life-reorganizing plan, but in the end it hasn't changed a thing.

You may have even thought of just giving up— deciding that society is too sick to bother adjusting to.

The idea of going to some sort of counselor or therapist is probably way down on your list, if it's there at all. For one thing, most young people don't realize that such help is available. Or if they do know, they reject it because they think it has to be expensive (untrue) or because they believe the old wives' tales that range from "You've got to be crazy

21

to see a shrink" to "Therapy destroys your creativity—if not your soul."

This book will tell you who gives professional help and how, and what it can and can't accomplish. And today there is a great deal of creative, hassle-free help available for people who are smart enough to seek it out and sane enough to use it.

But before that, let's clear up the myths and stereotypes about therapy that have kept so many people from trying it.

Seven Old Wives' Tales

1. "You have to be crazy to go to a shrink."

This, your basic old wives' tale, is only a slight improvement over equating emotional problems with possession by demons. Fortunately, people are beginning to realize now that even the sanest, healthiest among them develop problems. It's helping, too, that more and more public figures, from sports stars to major politicians, are owning up to getting therapy.

In fact, the kind of person most likely to benefit from therapy is not the basket case, but someone young, active, intelligent, involved in life, and searching for a kind of liberation.

2. "Going for therapy shows you're giving up."

On the contrary. It takes brains and energy—and

considerable optimism—to go to the trouble of seeking out the best help. Moreover, going for therapy shows you believe in yourself; a commitment to self-improvement and a willingness to deal with your problems instead of just licking your wounds is scarcely a cop-out.

3. "People who go for therapy have some special needs that other people don't have."

It's not that their needs are different or more extensive. It's more likely that their normal needs have been thwarted so often that either they feel unhappy a lot, or they can't seem to succeed at what matters to them.

Of course, that also describes plenty of people who will never bother to see a therapist. You could say that a person in therapy is different (and luckier) because that person is aware of feeling cramped or stymied, and smart enough to know that he can't fix it on his own.

4. "It's safer to suffer."

Most of us ignore a problem until we can't any longer; it's much easier that way. The prospect of change is frightening—even when that change would certainly be an improvement.

Amanda, for instance, always has to make herself a buffoon. She just can't play it straight, because the groans, the cries of "Oh, cut it out, Amanda," and the occasional laughs she gets at school are at least, as she puts it, "Some proof that people know I'm there." Her style is also a way of keeping people at a distance, avoiding the challenge and responsibility of the friendships she might develop if she were to drop her clown act. Amanda scoffs at the idea of therapy. "Who needs it?" she says. "Watch me slip on this imaginary giant banana peel! Whoops!"

5. "Problems are what make you interesting." "If we didn't have problems, what else would we talk about?"

Marty laughed as she launched into a gleeful recitation of her latest suicidal dream. She and her friends spend hours discussing one another's inner turmoil—not really in an effort to solve their problems, but rather to fondle, compare, and admire them like new motorcycles or suede boots. Marty's clique has made emotional distress into a kind of status symbol; a necessary credential of "inner depth" and sensitivity. Actually, hang-ups have a way of plugging up "inner depths" rather than creating them. Working on solving problems doesn't make you vapid and shallow; on the contrary, it can give you a chance to see that you are more complex and interesting than you ever seriously suspected.

6. "Therapy is bad for the soul."

The media delight in portraying the psychiatrist

as a stiff and humorless egghead, determined to prune back your poetic nature, lop off your charming eccentricities, and fit you squarely into society's mold.

The truth is that no decent therapist is out to make you behave or conform. The therapist is not pushing any particular life-style or any values you don't find compatible. The person is there to help you become as much YOU as possible, to help you get out from under the hang-ups that are keeping you from getting what you really want in life.

7. "Going to a therapist implies a long, drawn-out commitment."

It doesn't have to! Sometimes one or two sessions are all you need to sort things out. Ironically, the people who shy away from therapy because they think you can't accomplish anything in less than *years* of treatment are occasionally the ones who turn instead to some popular religious cult for "answers." (What they don't realize is that the Asian monks who get something out of the chanting and other rituals have put in a lifetime of learning and discipline to get there!)

So many people are able to get the therapy help they need in a brief period of a session or two, that some clinics operate almost exclusively on that basis.

Who "needs" therapy? Who can use it? And just how badly do you have to need it to ask for some?

You're surprised to learn that Charlie is seeing a shrink. He seems so totally normal. You wonder why Jill, who hops from bed to bed, doesn't go to one. If you had to decide which of your friends "ought" to be in therapy, it wouldn't be easy.

It's hard to judge the intensity of someone else's personal distress, or his wish to improve. Despite appearances, Charlie may be very unhappy, or he may be in a temporary quandary and aware that you don't have to wait until your chin is dragging in the dust before you go for help. Jill, on the other hand, may be too frightened—or too apathetic—to seek more productive ways of coping with her anxiety. Even stress that not too many other people have to face doesn't necessarily call for therapy. Amy's parents' divorce is certainly an upheaval, but after fifteen years of listening to them screaming and threatening to kill each other, it may be more of a relief than a tragedy.

If it's hard to tell about other people, it's even harder to tell about yourself. First of all, everyone—without exception—feels anxious and miserable some of the time. It would be strange *not* to feel terrible if, for example, the new French teacher put you down in front of the entire class for no reason. Not only are there random tragedies and everyday stresses that can bring on anxiety, but adolescence itself is a time when many people feel uptight and miserable.

It is, after all, a fairly momentous transition time. Not only are you facing all kinds of new responsibilities and pressures and worries about your future, you also have to do your best to grasp and define what there is about you that is constant and unwaveringly YOU amidst so much change and turmoil and an array of moods that seem to careen from one extreme to another. At best, it's a quirky, troublesome period. If the adults around are too preoccupied with their own problems or are stifling you or just don't seem to understand you, it's very depressing to have to sit in class day after day or at the dinner table night after night.

The fact is, we can all cope with *some* distress and confusion, loss, betrayal, fear, and pressure. It's when those things exceed our ability to cope efficiently that we run amok. Then the pain, like some blob in a horror movie, isn't destroyed, but grows all kinds of extra parts and tentacles. We have all sorts of ways of beating the system, skirting the problem, ambushing the blob and killing it. Sometimes some ways work better than others. Here are some of the most popular.

- *Denial.* When you will not or cannot deal with stress or emotional pain, you may be inclined to deny it, wish it away, just pretend that it doesn't exist. But the problem is often undeterred by your snub; it only becomes more insidious: sneakier, harder to reach, *more* pressing—and harder ultimately to cope with.

• *Escape.* Some people respond to overstress by fleeing—or trying to flee—into a high or a drunken stupor, a mad, frenetic pace of activity, or just an unbelievable amount of sleep. But this approach tends to compound rather than eliminate the original problems.

• *Taking it out on your body.* Not too many people know that the body can be an all too convenient repository for the unacknowledged emotional dross that the mind is too chicken and/or too cleverly evasive to deal with.

If you are skeptical about the whole idea of unacceptable emotions turning up in physical form, remember that attack of stomach butterflies and/or diarrhea before you had to speak to the entire student body, or those headaches you get when your father starts in about your boyfriend.

Those mini-symptoms—which a lot of us get from time to time—are just tiny ephemeral versions of much bigger, grander physical complaints: an ulcer, colitis, chronic constipation, nausea and vomiting,

severe menstrual cramps, heart palpitations or shortness of breath for no reason, and certain skin condi-
tions. Any of these ailments can be psychosomatic.

A psychosomatic symptom, by the way, is *not*
the same as an imaginary symptom. A psychosomatic symptom is clearly there—actual and observ-
able. A psychosomatic ulcer is just as real and raw
and painful as a wholly organically caused one; the
only difference is that a psychosomatic ulcer has
been aggravated or perhaps even caused by emotional stress.

Why do we sometimes use our bodies to express
our emotional pain? Well, it's got to come out somewhere. A girl who feels emotionally "crushed" and
"pressured" or "suffering under a terrible weight"
might feel it in her shortness of breath or skipped
heartbeats, because she cannot face it in her head.
Similarly, repressed anger, for example, might come
out in chronic, explosive diarrhea. Throwing up or
stomach cramps might be a person's very literal way
of expressing a forbidden thought such as, "I just
can't stomach the way my parents are treating me."
Frequent colds or anything in the respiratory area
might represent a disguised way of crying, what
with all the sniffling and choking, the red nose and
running eyes. And those are just a few!

Obviously, any physical ailment should be taken
first to a regular doctor, even if you have good reason to suspect an emotional connection.

Taking it out on yourself or others

Some of our buried needs and wishes manage to express themselves not in a physical pain or ailment but in behavior that seems to go absolutely counter to our conscious intentions. Haven't you ever done something for which you felt like kicking yourself? Or wished you could vanish into the bowels of the earth for blurting out something unthinkable?

Perhaps that is happening to you on a regular basis; those buried, disowned feelings keep burbling up unexpectedly, making you say and commit incredible gaucheries. Nobody likes to be pushed around from inside—nor to have to go around muttering, "I'm so sorry," and "Why did I do that?" and feeling helpless and clumsy all the time. It's scary having to wonder just how far this weird, angry person inside is going to push you.

Acting out your unacknowledged inner pain can take a simpler form, like Connie's chronic inability to be on time. Perhaps, since Connie is exceedingly soft-spoken and gentle, it is the only way she can dare to give in to her wish to control the people around her.

Or like Wally, who will work hard at a summer job, be praised for it, and then, invariably, do something outrageous, like not showing up for work at all the last week, to cancel out his success. Wally always comes on strong with a new girl, until she shows signs of really liking him, at which point he starts acting strange and distant.

Wally suffers, in the opinion of one therapist, from a condition known as "anticipatory creephood," a conviction that he is rotten to the core. In fact, he is competent, talented, and bright. But, since he's convinced that he is bound to fail sooner or later, he does it to himself to avoid the anxiety of waiting around until it happens. With a therapist, Wally could begin to work on seeing himself, clay feet and all, as a worthy person. All sorts of interesting things might happen to Wally if he'd let them.

Then there is Jason, who is even more devious about making things bad for himself. Jason has a genius for making other people feel small and stupid. It's not that he really feels superior to everyone else; on the contrary, the putdowns are just his crude defense against a fear that everyone would dump on *him* if he gave them half a chance. But the price, for Jason, is unbearable loneliness.

Many of us devote a lot of energy to keeping our fears, our illegitimate anger, and various yearnings out of sight, and presumably out of mind. We assume that our needs just can't be met; that we have a lot of nerve even wanting what we want.

But the feelings come through despite our attempts to censor them, and we end up paying a heavy price for having forced underground those wishes that we've judged unacceptable. In therapy,

Jason—if he were interested—could probably discover and come to terms with his feelings of unworthiness, instead of continuing to keep them under wraps where they run his life, keep him bitter, and wreck his chances for venturing into the warm relationships he secretly craves.

Sometimes, wishes—bound and gagged inside of us, but potent nonetheless—manage to screw things up on a much grander scale: reckless driving, drug taking, dropping out of school. Some people act destructively towards others rather than themselves: setting fires, stealing, breaking windows may feel like a release to them. Such behavior can mask a person's inner anxiety so well that he isn't at all interested in changing.

It may sound contradictory, but if you are more inclined to make yourself the victim, you're actually in a lot better shape. You're probably hurting, and consequently much closer to recognizing that something is wrong—and closer to doing something about it.

What about the person who can say, "I'm bugged, all right, but you would be too if you were in my shoes. I'm living in a snake pit at home . . . or my father's in jail . . . or I've got to live with this very serious physical handicap."

These are all externals, all right, but if any outside misery is causing you inside anguish, it may still be worth seeking assistance in getting a handle on coping with it. It doesn't matter whether your pain is "justified" by outside circumstances. What's important is whether the outside event or situation has—even temporarily—immobilized your coping apparatus. Only you can really determine that.

If you had some persistent, annoying stomach cramps which weren't killing you but were bothering you, you'd go to a doctor to check it out, right? So why not do the same for emotional pain?

What is therapy supposed to accomplish?

Whether they're tangible or not, each person has private goals, but here are some of the kinds of results that people in therapy might realistically hope to achieve.

1. *Stopping your pain.* Therapy can make you start feeling good (and feeling safe and happy about it instead of guilty or apprehensive); it can help you to no longer have to put up with self-punishing physical discomfort or repeated injuries, or any of the miseries that disguise emotional conflict. Sometimes therapy can do wonders where a medical approach to a physical problem has failed. Therapy can help you get rid of a specific irrational fear that has been a secret embarrassment and has kept you from traveling or dating more or enjoying any number of things. It can help you to feel human again, because you are freed from an over-

whelming panic or depression or sense of helplessness.

In therapy, the more of your feelings you can express in words, the less those feelings are going to need to find their own outlets and pop out with potentially embarrassing or painful consequences for you. Therefore, when you learn to recognize and talk about your own feelings, you become the driver and the navigator once again, instead of the blindfolded, cowering passenger.

2. *Learning to like yourself better.* This is something that many people find in therapy—even if they weren't particularly and specifically seeking it. Learning to like yourself better doesn't come from neatly removing all your faults, all the little things you dislike about yourself. Rather, it comes from a new acceptance of yourself.

As the therapist encourages you to let your most embarrassing feelings surface, they finally see the light of day; and *they* are seen, not as bad or as foolish, but as signals, expressions of needs and desires that you had not, up until now, been able to recognize. But when you see them, you can quit stepping on your own toes, call off the sabotage. Make friends with yourself.

In the process, of course, you learn that you aren't perfect and never will be (despite all those furious attempts to "shape up"), but you also learn that you're really a lot more lovable than you thought.

3. *New tools for living.* You don't have to be looking for a specific remedy to a specific hang-up; you may be looking toward the future, wanting to clarify hazy feelings or to explore new, powerful good feelings. You may want to learn the best way to recognize and use the strength that you have inside you—to be the most competent, the most productive, and the most loving YOU that you possibly can.

None of these various reasons—or goals—for seeking help is mutually exclusive. Each good result tends to enhance and reinforce others; you might conceivably get more out of therapy than you ever really expected.

Do you have to be able to tell the reason that you've come?

Not at all; nor is it always possible to do so. Many people have something concrete they can pin the rap on (which may or may not be what's *really* troubling them), but even without a nifty, coherent answer, you're entitled to the therapist's time and attention.

Feelings are elusive and not always so easy to recognize. If, for example, you consciously or unconsciously resent your sister but fear the force of your bitterness, you might turn the anger inward and feel "just numb" and out of it, unable to concentrate, or, perhaps, "empty and hungry all the time."

Some apparent problems aren't the real thing at all; they are the result of an attempt to avoid dealing with a deeper problem. Take drugs, for example. Barring medical complications, many therapists do not consider drug abuse the problem, but rather the person's faulty attempt to get rid of the problem. Instead of harping on the drug-taking specifics, a good therapist would probably concentrate on helping a young person learn better ways of dealing with the pain he's using drugs to escape from.

Some people can't cite anything specific. They just feel bored with everything, or lonely and isolated, or panicky and alarmed, or listless and confused—for no apparent reason. Any similar distress is perfectly okay for a place to start. As one therapist puts it, "I don't treat problems; I treat people."

Why do some people go—and get turned off immediately?

Some people make an appointment or get as far as the therapist's door and then don't follow through. That's often because they have not come under their own steam. Unlike a pill that can be shoved down someone's throat, therapy has to be taken willingly, or it is useless. If you are pushed into it, you may be so turned off that you may never want to go on your own.

It's not essential that you be the one to decide that you will go in the first place; some people do need to be led by the hand (or gently pushed), and it may be more comfortable that way. But you know better than anyone else whether you hurt or not, and it can be a drag to wait for somebody else to take the initiative for you.

No matter whose idea it is to go, the important thing is getting active in therapy. Psychologist Gordon Allport once described therapy as a process of growing muscles where we once had injuries. If you know anything about muscle-building, then you know that you can't develop muscles by just having someone else massage or pummel you. In therapy, too, the therapist is there to coach you in your working-out endeavor, but the flexing and the stretching have got to be entirely yours. So—once the ice is broken and your therapy has gotten going, you must be the moving force behind it.

What if you think you only need a little bit of help— what if you aren't quite ready for a shrink?

There are resources—right in your own community, at school and over the phone. There are people who can help you up to a point, and refer you, if you like, to a bona fide shrink. Hotlines and peer counseling are the newer modes of help; doctors, clergypeople, and guidance counselors are the more traditional. Anyway, they're sources of help that shouldn't be overlooked.

2

Help-without having to go to the shrink

Saving face: how much help in a hotline?

You may have phoned a hotline once or twice, or perhaps you've worked on one. Some hotlines offer everything from talking a caller out of attempting suicide to recommending a low-cost gynecologist. Other help-switchboards concentrate on a single difficulty—sexual hang-ups, family friction, or drug problems.

Some hotlines are very active and practical. The National Runaway Switchboard (800-621-4000, toll-free) in Chicago operates nationwide to aid runaway teenagers. The Switchboard will try to arrange for the caller to get practical assistance: transportation or a place to stay. They also can refer a caller to a wide variety of service agencies anywhere in the country.

Some hotlines are a great deal less ambitious,

seeking only to provide callers with a friendly voice, a word of cheer, and a helpful suggestion or two. But no matter how large or how limited their scope, hotlines do offer several unique advantages to their callers.

(1) *Odd hours/All hours.* Most hotlines operate, if not on a twenty-four-hour basis, at least during some evening or weekend hours, which fills a gap for people who simply aren't able to schedule their crises and problems from nine to five.

(2) *Immediate access—no red tape.* Not only is there no charge for the service, there are no forms to fill out, no hassles getting there, and no need to accommodate yourself to someone's appointment calendar. You get right down to business, telling the person who answers exactly what the problem is.

(3) *Help.* You may need some information about whether your parents can legally force you to live at home, or whether you can get pregnant without intercourse, or how much masturbation is too much. Perhaps you need advice on how to deal with an alcoholic mother. The person answering will tell you what he or she can, but if your problems seem beyond the person, he's likely to offer you the name and number of a doctor, clinic, or agency.

If you have a pressing family problem, or a nameless panic that's got hold of you, or a sudden unendurable urge to do something violent, a hotline operator can bring you some calm, some hope, a feeling of support. The phone line can serve, quite literally, as a lifeline.

Who's there?

Some hotline staffers are actually professional therapists, working on a part-time volunteer basis. Others have been trained by professionals, but the amount and quality of their training can vary. (One suicide-prevention hotline in the East requires only a ten-hour course.) Unless you know how qualified the person to whom you are talking is, you are operating in the dark.

As fine and useful as hotlines are—and they are— they were never conceived to be a substitute for other kinds of help. Still, some people overuse or overestimate the hotline, finding its combination of (safe) distance and anonymity and intimacy appealing. You're connected, but you have the option of disappearing in one second flat.

Calling a hotline can certainly be a good way to let off steam. For someone who is impulsive, it is definitely better to talk to a hotline staffer about the urge to smash someone than to go ahead and do it. But if you find yourself becoming addicted to a hotline, you may do better to face a helper head-on. In other words, it's nice to be able to get a lift now and then when you need it—but think how much more freedom you'd have if you learned to drive!

Peer counselors: what can they do for you?

Ever since the big drugs-in-school epidemic of the late 1960s, peer counseling programs have been starting up. Some programs have more of a social-service orientation than a therapeutic one. At one high school in California, peer counselors sought to make friends with students who seemed lonely. (Their effort made the whole place a lot friendlier.) At another school, in New York, peer counselors intervened effectively in potentially explosive situations between members of rival gangs or in student/teacher/administration conflicts.

Another program, in Pennsylvania, focused on personal counseling. Peer counselors spent many hours studying factual data on drugs, for example—reading extensively, visiting drug rehab centers, and interviewing doctors and ex-addicts. Then they offered information to their fellow students. They also operated a "rap room," in which kids could discuss problems they had at home or at school.

Their third function, and an important one, was as a referral service. The counselors knew when they were unable to help a fellow student, at which point they referred him to professional help through a highly selective list of local resources. According to Dr. Norman A. Sprinthall of the University of Minnesota, who designed a special high school course in the Psychology of Counseling, "trained peer counselors can be a very good resource, not only as a liaison between the kids and the authorities; nor just as a source of information and/or referral. They can also be a tremendous help in 'breaking the ice' for students who have anxieties but need a little convincing that there isn't anything shameful about seeking help."

As for the counseling discussions themselves, they may be fruitful. But what's even more likely is that, as a result of the open discussion, it may become obvious to the student being counseled that he's got a problem that can't really be handled in a peer setting.

Even with tremendous motivation and great natural talent, peer counselors aren't qualified to do full-fledged therapy—no matter how "professionally" they might represent themselves and their services. In fact, the best—and the best-trained—peer counselors are frequently the most realistic about their own limitations as substitute therapists.

The Daddy People

What about your doctor?

Doctors, to many of us, are the quintessential daddy-people: experts with a wonderful blend of science and homey wisdom. But when it comes to personal problems, it doesn't always work out that way.

That's not to say that you shouldn't go to your doctor; on the contrary, if your distress has any physical aspect whatsoever, you ought to check with a medical doctor before you look for a therapist. Extreme weight loss or fatigue or a persistent headache may indicate something organic. In fact, a responsible therapist wouldn't begin to treat someone with a physical complaint unless the person had already been checked out by a physician.

A kind and sensitive physician—and particularly one who has had more than perfunctory exposure to the idea of psychotherapy—will always take the time to find out how his patients feel—emotionally. If he can't find any reason for a teenager's severe stomach pains, he doesn't dismiss the patient, saying, "you're fine," implying that she oughtn't to take her little problems so seriously. Instead he will give her a chance to talk. Perhaps the girl will finally disclose, say, an abortion several months ago that she feels guilty about, or the fact that an older sister, many years ago, died at the same age from a kidney disease.

According to the director of one medical clinic, a great many people who say they've come in for medical reasons are actually seeking something non-medical such as counseling for drug problems or sexual problems or problems with their parents. Unfortunately, not all doctors have the time or the interest to uncover—much less treat—emotional upsets. For every Marcus Welby, there's a doctor who sees each patient as a collection of parts and pieces. Some die-hards who consider a problem hogwash if it can't be seen or felt or x-rayed may be grudging about recommending a therapist, even when asked.

Happily, the trend is changing dramatically; an aware and sympathetic physician can give you a great deal of authoritative—and reassuring—information, and that may be all you'll need to ease your mind. Beyond that, the doctor may be able to help you determine whether a certain problem might better be discussed with a therapist (and if so, it is likely he can steer you to a good one).

Your guidance counselor: (don't knock it if you haven't tried it)

They range from the inaccessible to the over-zealous—with many, many in between who are flexible, wise, and competent. Actually, guidance counselors are portrayed either as some sort of Magic Mr. Fix-it (for anything from acne to delinquency), or else they are *way* underestimated: wrongly written off as (1) harried clerks, buried under a pile of official records and forms; (2) quasi-cops who are supposed to mete out punishment for whispering in class or throwing pickles in the lunchroom; (3) spies who are there to find out about every kid's immoral activities; or (4) people who will see you once in your senior year to give you the word on whether you should apply to Yale—or automechanic school.

Obviously, when a guidance counselor has to be responsible for vocational and college advice to 500 or 1000 students (and/or a lot of clerical and disciplinary chores), he or she is not going to have much time—or taste—for chatting about a personal problem. Yet, many guidance counselors *do* have that capacity, at least within certain limits.

A counselor can console a girl who's hysterical and feels like a failure because she didn't make cheerleader . . . or listen to a boy who's upset and bitter because his father is hitting the bottle or his mother is fooling around. A counselor can't treat a drug problem singlehandedly or even agree to keep a student's confessed addiction a secret. ("That wouldn't be doing the student a favor anyway," one counselor says. "I wouldn't lie to him, I'd tell him that I could help him better by telling someone else.")

A counselor can't fill in gaps of love and/or structure in the lives of the students—nor can he or she try to scrutinize the sea of faces in the assembly hall for signs of neurosis. However, the counselor can generally let kids know that he is available to them, not just in the office by appointment, but in the hallways, in the cafeteria, and at games.

A counselor can't practice therapy, but he or she

can make referrals to professional therapists, usually offering a few different possibilities in order to give the student a choice.

The Clergyperson: pros and cons

Some years ago, a United States government survey showed that of all the adults in this country who sought professional help for a personal problem, 42 percent—the largest segment—went to a clergyman. It's logical when you think of it: the church, in most circles, is a more socially acceptable, more traditional and obvious place to turn to than a strange, alien place like a therapist's office, where "no one in the family has ever been before."

There is also a feeling that even if you practically never go to church, you are still connected with your clergyman, which means that he is responsible for you as one of his woolly flock. He's a professional good guy, right on hand.

Some clergymen are very good at counseling for emotional problems, but not all clergymen are equally good. One not so good clergyman might make someone feel terribly guilty—like George, who sought help for a sexual problem, only to be told that he was sinful and in need of penitence.

Or the clergyman might be ponderous and frustrating: if you were deeply disturbed about your inability to get along with your parents, it wouldn't do you much good to be told that they were your parents, after all, and you'd just have to accept that and get along with them.

What makes the difference? "The distinction," says Dr. Donald Smith, President of the American Association of Pastoral Counselors, "lies in the clergyman's training and experience as well as his personality." Cautioning against the "over-flamboyant type" or "anyone who claims to be able to effect an instant cure," Dr. Smith thinks that a clergyman is more likely to be an effective counselor if he has a willingness and capacity to care. "It is best if he has been in therapy himself, as that may help him understand better the difficulties involved in the process of opening up to another person."

Supervising Pastoral Counselor William Brockman of the Institutes of Religion and Health in New York is "amazed and impressed" at the sensitivity and skill of many young clergymen today, all over the country—in cities, towns, and rural areas. "They understand the psychological as well as the spiritual dimension in man," he says. "Consequently, they do not become anxious and fall back on the ritual of the church; they are able to approach a person's problem in a respectful and cautious way."

Not all clergy fill the bill themselves, but most will know of a pastoral counselor in your area. This is a person who has had extensive training in therapy; he is a specialist and not in competition with your own clergyman. If you are afraid that your own pastor would be offended at being bypassed in your search for counseling, you can write directly to the American Association of Pastoral Counselors and ask for a local referral. (See Chapter 10.)

The thing is this: not all the professional helpers around you are automatically qualified to offer the help you're looking for. If there's a doctor, a pastor, a teacher, or a school counselor you trust who has the time and the inclination to help you sort things out, by all means, give him or her a try. But if that one source or another doesn't come up to your expectations, it's nice to know that it isn't the end of the road—not by a long shot.

3

Therapists and counselors

Where does a therapist practice?

In a great variety of places! It might be in a suite in a plush apartment house, or a walk-in center in an old frame house with comfortable old chairs and a cat snoozing in one of them. Or it might be in a drab, paint-peeling room in the basement of a church. Whatever, the prestige of the location, the charm (or lack of it) has nothing at all to do with the quality of the therapy. In fact, some of the most expensive and successful private therapists give part of their time to clinic work at little or no cost to the clients.

Moreover, you can't judge the way a shrink thinks by the professional habitat: the same therapist might be dividing time between a hospital and a family counseling center; a runaway house and a university health service; or a private practice in the suburbs and a street clinic in the middle of a heavy drug-dealing neighborhood. Some of them even work in bus terminals and playgrounds—out in the street wherever young people are needing them. In fact, therapists and counselors are turning up in so many different settings (and traveling among them) that the chances are there is *someone* available to you without a very long wait, a high fee, or a great distance to travel.

Who is a therapist?

Do they have to be professionals? Some people would argue that "natural" therapists and counselors (i.e. nonprofessional ones not yet dehumanized by any accreditation) are better than the degree-laden variety. After all, they remind us, back at the Woodstock Festival in the hippies' heyday, it was members of a far-out commune called the Hog Farm who were helping terrified kids to come down from bad trips—while psychiatrists stood around, impressed, and unable to do half what the Hog Farmers were accomplishing. In fact, even though most hotlines and crisis centers are professionally run right now, the whole spirit behind them and the basic concept was as a kind of humanitarian alternative for kids who needed help but didn't want to have anything to do with oppressive establishment types.

Consequently, some of the newer, more radical, and innovative help centers are committed to "demystifying" the counseling process; to making it unawesome, unintimidating, and, thus, more palatable to the young. Some, in fact, go so far as to let untrained people do actual counseling—as if, just because someone happened to be an ex-addict or a former runaway, that person was automatically qualified to counsel others. (In one case at least, the concept backfired, when counselors at one clinic, whose *only* "qualifications" were having been addicts, were so long away from their drug experiences that the kids they were trying to counsel felt no rapport at all with them.)

You don't have to be stuffy to prefer
PROFESSIONAL help

It's true. Some of the most dynamic and aggressive movers in the mental health field—the least stuffy types you could find—are endorsing that notion. In fact, the directors of some help centers that are virtual models of relevance and hassle-free counseling insist on heavy professional training and experience in the counselors they hire.

It's not that they think the training *creates* good counselors; it's just that the lack of adequate training ("even in a very accurately empathetic, open, honest individual") can be a handicap. Creative listening, as we have been saying, is more than a warmhearted impulse; it is a skill that is never quickly or easily acquired.

Andy Kane and Alan Reed, directors of the very excellent—and un-put-offish—Counseling Center in Milwaukee, point out some of the disadvantages of using untrained or minimally trained counselors. They cite the example of a guy who is severely depressed. The counselor who means well but has had no real substantial background in counseling says, after a session with the depressed guy, "Oh, I can feel that I really helped him," not realizing that the "good" counseling session has merely allowed the depressed guy to gather up enough energy to go ahead and actually kill himself (something he'd thought about but had been too depressed to actually do before).

In addition, Kane and Reed have found that the professional counselor is much more likely than the nonprofessional to understand that he is there to help the counselee get better as opposed to *making* the counselee get better. This acquired skill of the counselor's—to keep his own ego out of the therapy —not only allows him to develop a close helping relationship with the counselee, but also makes him able to "step back and make referrals when appropriate, rather than being so personally involved that he gets angry at the counselee for not getting better."

At the Counseling Center, Kane and Reed have found simply that "the professionally trained counselor does a better job of offering the help needed by the people coming to us for counseling."

Not every crisis or problem is going to require professional help; yours might respond beautifully to the efforts of a peer counselor, for example, or even the "counseling" of some gentle person that you happen to meet at the zoo. But if you've already tried that route and/or just because you do have the *option*, you might want to consider the fact that there really are good reasons to seek out either a professional or at least a well-trained paraprofessional with some professional backup behind him.

Professional therapists: who are they?

A varied lot, to say the least; their training and backgrounds, goals, and techniques may vary enormously! Still, they share a basic belief in the value of therapy.

Are they all psychiatrists?

Psychiatrists represent only a small fraction of all the therapists practicing in this country. A psychiatrist, just for the record, is a doctor of medicine who—instead of handing out Band-Aids, swabbing throats, or snatching out appendixes—specializes in *mental* health. Up until the Second World War, psychiatrists had the therapy field pretty much to themselves; but the war itself brought on such a tremendous new demand for therapy that social workers and clinical psychologists were invited to join the club, so to speak. As licensed medical doctors, psychiatrists are the only kind of psychotherapists who can legally prescribe drugs, but they are by no means the only ones who can provide first-rate therapy.

Is there any difference between the kind of therapy you'd get from a psychiatrist, a psychologist, and a social worker?

This question has produced some of the liveliest debates between the group that insists that the better therapists of all three professions have more in common than *not* in common, and the group that maintains that there *is* a difference, and that one kind or another is clearly superior to the others.

If you've dealt with any therapists in the past, you may well have your own feelings on the matter. Here are some of the things that some of *them* have expressed.

The psychiatrist: who he is and isn't

In cartoons, he usually has a pointed beard and a Viennese accent: very formal and uptight. In real life, the stereotype is no truer than saying that all housewives resemble Betty Crocker. Depending on where he's practicing, in fact, a psychiatrist is as likely to be wearing faded blue jeans as "Establishment" clothes.

A psychiatrist's training is very extensive (a minimum of seven years after college—and some specialists known as psychoanalysts almost seem to spend more years in training than they have left to practice when they finish!). You might think that that would train the humanness right out of them, but fortunately it doesn't usually work that way at all. Even while that long and arduous training goes on and on —and even though it stresses detachment and a hounddog's determination to dig, dig, dig into a person's past in order to understand and work on current problems—still . . . it's been observed that most young psychiatrists are coming out unjaded and eager and with a great deal of compassion as well as professional commitment toward the people who come to them for help.

The fact that a psychiatrist's fee can run up to $35, $50, or $100 for an hour's session makes some people think that a psychiatrist is out to make a bundle. Actually, when you compare what he makes to, say a dermatologist—who may or may not charge as much for an appointment but who can treat many patients (each of whom is paying) within an hour's time—you can see that money is obviously not the psychiatrist's primary concern. Also, many psychiatrists donate at least a portion of their time to clinic work without pay; and many therapists—psychiatrists included—will adjust their fee downwards for a person who can't afford the usual rate.

The psychologist: out of his lab

The popular stereotypes are (1) a fellow in a white coat, fiendishly sending weary white rats through ever more confusing mazes, and (2) a human computer who goes around assigning IQ scores on the basis of how fast you can string some beads.

It is true that psychologists have to have had extensive academic training (an M.A. if not a Ph.D.), and that may well have included a certain amount of animal behavior research. As far as the testing goes, the psychologist is top dog, since psychologists alone are *the* professional group allowed to give and evaluate mental tests.

But before he can become a therapist, a psychologist must also have had at least two years of supervised experience in therapy, so that by the time he gets to you, he is liberated from the graphs and jargon, the chalk dust, and the rodents. In fact, one quite prominent psychologist we know is so mellow that he laughs and cries along with his clients.

Psychologists are said to differ from psychiatrists in their approach to emotional problems. They look at problems not as the result of an early unhappy experience, but as a failure in learning. Presumably, psychologists are more inclined to try to get you to modify your behavior directly, while psychiatrists will want you to look into the early roots and shoots of the problem. Actually, there is no such clear-cut distinction: each individual has his or her own technique or combination of techniques—or a whole bag of *different* techniques for responding to individual clients and their individual problems.

The social worker: "with an eye on the environment"

While many social workers deal largely with the practical and economic problems of their clients, some are engaged primarily or exclusively in psychotherapy. Of those, some claim that they are just like other therapists, while others insist that they are *more* so; that is, that social workers alone are the therapists with a realistic approach to problems. As one social worker/therapist says, "We are very much concerned with finding out what makes a person tick: his strengths as well as his weaknesses; however, we practice therapy with a little extra attention to environmental problems that might be contributing to a client's difficulty."

What this means, she explains, is that if a boy is having trouble at school, for example, "a psychologist or psychiatrist would probably go about trying to find out what's wrong with the boy while *we* would look for relationships between that boy and his surroundings." Rather than treating a client in a vacuum, she says, a social worker as therapist will sometimes even try to manipulate "a troublesome outside reality."

She found, for example, that students at a certain high school where she was a consultant were having an enormous upsurge of emotional tension and problem behavior at lunchtime: some were sick to their stomachs, others fought viciously, still others were overwrought, depressed, or in tears.

The problem, that social worker determined, was largely because the lunchroom in the school was hopelessly overcrowded, shrill, depressing, and "a degrading, upsetting situation." She managed to relieve a lot of the distress by getting the school to cut out lunchhour and end the school day earlier.

Social workers are sometimes accused of being superficial in their therapy. Some argue that it isn't true at all, that people only have that impression because social work training is generally shorter than that of other therapists, and, consequently, the field just has less snob appeal than psychology or psychiatry. They are quick to point out that social work training is entirely people-oriented right from the very first year, not "cluttered" up with months or years of academic and/or medical training. The other side answers the charge by agreeing: "Well, listen, if we make surface changes that are going to make a person more comfortable in his life, is that really so bad?"

Counselors

There's still more! To meet the leaping, bounding demand for professional help in recent years, certain other professions have been allowed to join the ranks of the therapist stronghold.

Among the best-trained, best-qualified, and most rigorously screened of these "others" are members of some of the counseling professions which have developed and grown in such a way as to blur the already hazy line between traditional *counseling* and *therapy*. (Counseling is presumed to be involved with here-and-now issues that the person being counseled is already aware of, while therapy deals with, as you have no doubt already gathered, the not-so-easily-accessible things. Therapy may emphasize the past and the unconscious as good sources of insight into what's going on presently.)

Pastoral counselors

As we said, every pastor is a counselor and can say so—in good faith! But not all of them are equally good at it. If you want to be sure you're talking to the right kind, it's nice to know that there is a whole separate profession known as pastoral counseling. The training (beyond seminary experience) consists of a lot of psychotherapeutic theory, method, and practice, and clinical experience under the supervision of psychiatrists, psychologists, and senior pastoral counselors. The result, according to Pastoral Counselor Brockman, has been "a growing number of clergymen equipped to do significant in-depth psychotherapy."

Iona College is just one of several institutions with a graduate program in pastoral counseling. "Historically," their brochure states, "the pastoral counselor was concerned with giving spiritual advice. . . . But as time went on, clergymen and religious leaders recognized that many of those seeking spiritual consolation were really in need of psychological counseling as a preparation for spiritual counseling and spiritual growth."

Just as the other kinds of therapists are alleged to have their own respective "slant" or emphasis, a pastoral counselor might be one who would consider any possible spiritual component of a person's distress. Says Pastor Brockman, "Depression may be a symptom of a psychological problem—or it may be an expression of a spiritual need, as in a wish to feel connected to a reality above and beyond oneself and one's neighbors."

Marriage and family counselors (also called couples counselors)

This group is a mixed bag in itself! Members of the American Association of Marriage and Family Counselors come from a variety of professional disciplines: they are psychologists, psychiatrists, pastoral counselors (the AAMFC and the American Association of Pastoral Counselors overlap to the tune of 25 percent in their memberships), and others with either a degree in counseling or a minimum of an M.A. in a field like sociology, plus at least two years of supervised clinical experience.

While these various marriage and family counselors can function as regular therapists, treating individuals, their special interest and perspective are likely to be the troubled relationships in a family or between a couple. The treatment goal might be to change a bad situation within a certain family . . . or it might simply be to help one member of the family to cope with all the craziness the others are handing out.

How can you tell which professional type is right for you?

It really may not matter. One therapist we know insists that when a therapist is "really tuned in," you can't tell which strain he comes from and you don't even care. What you want, this therapist insists, is someone with empathy, with respect for you, and with accurate understanding. That means someone who can really *hear what you are saying* as opposed to just "feeling along" with you as you unfold your tale.

Moreover, all sorts of journal articles state and

restate that it has yet to be proven that one type of professional training is better than the others for turning out good therapists. Some cynics say that it's because most of the subject matter taught to professionals is irrelevant to psychotherapy. Other people explain that success depends on the therapist's ability to establish just the right kind of relationship with his client, and that this particular knack is taught about equally well by the different disciplines.

You and the therapist: what is the relationship really *like?*

For starters, you can rightly assume that the therapist is on your side; he or she is not some authority figure challenging your right to think and feel and act the way you do. He is an advocate of yours, an ally. He's interested in you and your well-being— even if that means saying *some* things you aren't necessarily going to want to hear. In other words, as friendly and caring as the therapist is (and he is), he is *not* a Mr. Niceguy. He is not there to agree that the world has wronged you, *or* to give you wishy-washy, unconditional approval, *or* (worse yet) to smother you with a great show of affection and rollicking enthusiasm.

A good therapist conveys his concern with a low-key, perhaps wordless, assurance that he is committed to helping you—no matter how "outrageous" you think you are (or even try to prove you are).

Whether you've come to a fancy office, a clinic, or a crisis center, the therapist is most likely to view you *not* as a pathetic creature, but very much as a worthwhile person with the brains and the heart to want to master certain problems. He can't help but respect you.

The relationship with a therapist is really so different from what anyone is used to, it's hard to imagine it free of any misconceptions. Here are just a couple of them:

Don't therapists have to be free of any problems themselves in order to help someone else?

If that were a real criterion, there would be no therapists around—not even one! It is only human to have problems; mental health is not the absence of problems, it is being in touch with them, having a good method for coping with them. A well-trained and sensitive therapist has, one hopes, worked on himself enough in his own therapy so that he is not in danger of infecting you with his bugs, so to speak.

If a therapist is good, religion, political persuasion, ethnic background, age, or gender shouldn't make any difference in the quality or validity of the treatment you receive.

Of course, you might feel most comfortable with

a woman, a black, or a very young person, and that may strongly influence your choice of a therapist. There's nothing wrong with that. But just in case you aren't able to get exactly the model you had in mind, it is nice to know that a good therapist can understand your feelings no matter who he is: he doesn't have to *be* you to know you; the fact that he may be different from you is no barrier to his ability to feel with you.

Can't they read your mind? That would make a person feel so vulnerable!

If they could . . . it certainly would! Fortunately, they *can't* read minds, no matter how clever and wise and experienced they are. This particular misconception is surprisingly prevalent. Supposedly, the rumor goes, a trained therapist can psych you out as soon as you open your mouth, if he hasn't already done so by noting what you're wearing and how you're sitting and whether your eyes meet his without a lot of blinking and staring at your shoes. Will he sit there feeling superior while you feel naked and embarrassed, knowing he knows something you don't know (about you!)? Or will he be nice and tell you right away what it all "means," how this and that about you indicates craziness, etc., etc.

Therapists aren't smug little kids trying to get the goods on you; nor are they instantly aware of your secrets. Therapists are trained to pick up on the various nonverbal expressions you give out, as well as what you choose to tell them, but that is all there is to it. They *definitely* don't have x-ray vision, and they depend greatly on what *you* tell them.

Even if a therapist could give you an instant laundry list of what's wrong, it wouldn't be worth too much; even being told what's wrong and why won't automatically cure it. If your arm hurts because you broke it falling off a horse, it's good to *know* that, sure; but the information in itself isn't sufficient to make the arm better.

In fact, even Big Dramatic Insights that are handed to you—too soon, out of context—are never the ones that lead to spontaneous improvements in your life. The valuable insights have nothing to do with some outside person saying, "Aha, here's the cause of your discomfort"; the good ones are the ones that you ferret out yourself. The therapist is there to help you; to use all the skill he can to guide *you* in *your* quest. A famous choreographer compares a skilled therapist to a very resilient floor in a ballet studio on which you, the dancer, can improve your technique and learn a great deal without that floor having actually taught you anything.

*Your therapist: his special way of being
on your side*
- First of all, he can't be shocked. Be assured of

that! Nothing you have done or felt or said or thought or even contemplated can shock a professional therapist. He's heard it all before—in spades!

• As much as you tell him, and it may be more than you've ever told anyone else, your privacy remains intact. He's not going to tell your parents, your school, or anyone else; it's a matter of professional ethics *and* his own personal sense of honor.

• His interest in your secrets is strictly professional. You can compare baring your soul to the therapist to a woman allowing a gynecologist to examine her reproductive organs: he's doing it for your benefit, not for his kicks.

• He doesn't *have* to like you: many therapists will only work with patients they like, but one therapist we know tells his patients, "Don't depend on my liking you; I'm here to work my butt off to help you. Your growth is more important than our relationship."

• He doesn't make value judgments as such—but he's there to keep you from pulling the wool over your own eyes. If you tell him about some "awful" thing you've done or about something even more frightful that you have fantasies about doing, he sees those things not in a good/bad context, but as expressions of certain needs or desires that you have tried to keep yourself from feeling.

As for the most hostile—or obscene—*feelings* you may describe to him, he will most likely tell you

emphatically and repeatedly that imagining doing
something (no matter how appalling) is *entirely
blameless and in no way "almost the same as" doing
it.*

A special kind of objectivity

A therapist can point out how your father may not
really be so mindlessly cruel and unreasonable in
the way he treats you. The therapist isn't saying,
"Look, you stupid slob, you brought it on yourself,
ha ha!" But he might help you to see—from the way
you described the last few scenes and squabbles at
the dinner table—how you might have been subtly
antagonizing your father as you sat at the table
silently nursing your resentment over the *last* time
he was mean to you.

Even though your therapist is not going to dismiss
you as a devil or a rat for *whatever* you've done, his
very concern for you and interest in your welfare
compel him to be more than a soothing companion.
In short, he's not likely to let you get away with
rationalizing or trying to skip out on recognizing
what you are *really* up to. For example, when Terry
insisted that she had only gone to bed with the
creepy guy from the dance because she had smoked
pot first and wasn't responsible for what followed,
her therapist pointed out that Terry ought to realize
that she might have smoked the pot *in order* to abdicate any responsibility for what she wanted to do

(which was to sleep with the "creepy" guy). The therapist's concern wasn't with keeping Terry unbedded, but simply with helping her to get in touch with her feelings; to work on understanding why she needed so badly to disown her sexual feelings, why she could afford to express them only when she was high and "not herself."

*Don't you have to get very dependent
on your therapist?*

Never for keeps. Even on a temporary basis, it all depends. You can use a therapist or counselor in a relatively casual way as a sounding board or for a simple matter, and feel no more or less involved or grateful than you would feel about a dentist or a car mechanic or a hairdresser.

There *are*, however, many cases in which the therapist appears to temporarily take on great significance in a person's life. Even then, it's nothing to fear. Not only does it go away, but while it's there, it can do you a lot of good. It *doesn't* mean that you've become a helpless basket case; nor does it mean that you're falling in love with your shrink. What's happened is something known in the trade as "transference," a process in which the therapist appears to be looming very large in your life. Actually he has only become a handy flypaper for the same uncomfortable feelings that you had been harboring—consciously or not—towards close people like your parents or a brother. Here at last is a chance to recognize and deal with those feelings, and to free yourself so that the old buried fears and resentments and longings won't be able to screw up, confuse, and falsify relationships present and future.

It can feel pretty odd; it might seem to you as though you've developed a gigantic crush on the therapist—or wish that he were your parent because he seems so strong and perfect. On the other hand, you might find fault with "everything" about him, deciding that he's henpecked or sadistic. (And those strong feelings towards the therapist appear on the basis of really knowing almost nothing about him.)

The process can tune you in to understanding some obsolete but still rankling resentments—or unrequited tender feelings—from way back when, feelings which still account for present lumps and knots in your relationships.

What's the net result of all this transference? A more realistic and relaxed way of looking at—and treating—real people in the real world; it may feel like getting out from under a heavy, wet, smelly blanket.

It can feel embarrassing or frightening, especially when you don't know what's going on, or don't realize that it's normal, temporary, and very much a sign of progress. You may be tempted to keep those intense and seemingly excessive feelings to yourself.

But if you can resist that urge, you're way ahead of the game. The therapist *knows* not to take any of it personally. He will not be flattered or mad at you or think you're silly. Nor will he try to take advantage of it or you. He won't respond to any come-on, nor will he rise to even your best efforts to get his goat or put him down. He's trained to take that guff and to see it—quite properly—as grist for the mill, your mill.

4
What is therapy?

What is therapy, anyway?

Basically, it is a process in which you talk and someone listens. You talk freely and honestly about yourself and your feelings, and the therapist acts as a well-designed and sensitive sounding board, encouraging you to let it all out, offering support and helping you to really find out where you're coming from. Of course, in order to do this, you have to feel comfortable, and that takes shopping around.

What is the atmosphere like in therapy?
What are the rules of the game?

Some therapists allow and encourage their clients to move around, punch sofa pillows, curl up in a ball, scream, or get up and act out little scenes; others prefer that you sit and *talk* about any emotions you may be feeling strongly. Even among

73

those purists, some will use videotape regularly (but only with the client's approval) as an aid in helping clients to see themselves clearly. Others consider any electronic equipment to be artificial or intrusive.

Creative techniques are increasingly prevalent. One "interaction experience" is the teacup game invented by psychologist and author Dr. Thomas McGinnis. In this game, the client is asked to arrange a group of teacups to represent the members of his family. "Why did you put that one way over there?" Dr. McGinnis might ask. "How do you feel if I do this?" he asks, as he turns one cup upside down or places the daddy cup on top of one of the others.

Each therapist has his own policy on how much structure he thinks is important. Some thrive on informality and impose virtually no rules at all, while others are fairly strict.

The more formal types may end each session exactly on schedule, no matter what (even if no one else is waiting), while others might encourage you to stay and talk if you happen to be in the middle of something important. Some therapists let you call up a lot between appointments to ask questions or tell them nonemergency things; and/or they'll freely give you extra appointments on a spur-of-the-moment basis. Other ones might insist that you stick to the mutually agreed upon schedule in order to give the treatment a sense of order, a consistent and regular shape. (To insure that, they might ask you to pay for any appointment that you break without a pretty good reason.)

Some therapists ask you not to smoke or eat while you are there (while you are there they want you to be working on your anxiety, not soothing it). But others offer refreshments.

Don't be too hasty in rejecting a strict therapist

Some people definitely thrive on the freer kind of therapy environment, with the type of therapist who'll come out from behind his desk and hold your hand. But many others find they feel better—and are more able to be open—in a relatively contained and structured setup—it's like insurance against all that inner chaos tumbling out of you and taking over!

How long does therapy take?

That can vary, even assuming that you're in good shape to start with. Sometimes all you need are a couple of sessions to blow off steam or clarify something or shake off a momentary feeling of gloom or panic. At the opposite end, the *longest* kind of treatment available for a person who is healthy and functioning well, but still has problems and a wish to work them out, is a process known as psycho-analysis. This is an intensive (several days a week) job lasting from two to five years or longer. Such a major undertaking requires more time and money, and more patience, effort, and stability than most people are free to invest; in other words, only very few people are up to it. Anyway, you can see that it makes no sense to try to determine the severity of a person's problems by noting how long or how often the person goes to a therapist.

The short haul: brief therapy

Let's assume that, like most of us, you're planning on something at the shorter end. Fine. Even in just a few sessions, a good therapist can offer genuine and lasting results.

What can therapy do for you in a current crisis?

Let's say there's real trouble within or without, and you feel that you are falling apart. It may be an emergency—or it may only feel that way to you. At any rate, there are agitating times when everyone needs to share that pain, to talk to someone right away.

Maybe you've run away from home or your brother's been arrested; perhaps there's been a death in the family or someone is dying and throwing everyone else into a state of chaos and grief.

Perhaps the crisis is something personal, like a terribly strong wish to end it all (with just a trace of doubt that you really want to) or a nameless panic that's been licking at your heels, but now threatens to swallow you.

You feel like you need to be rescued, taken care

of; but if the therapist were *only* to take you under his wing like a little lost bird and promise to make everything okay, it would simply confirm your feelings now of total helplessness. Instead, a counselor or therapist would be sympathetic and reassuring, but he would also be doing his best to help *you* to mobilize your own best and strongest resources for meeting and coping with the stress.

He might try to help you understand this crisis in the context both of your general life situation (school, work, family, dating, and so on) and of any past crisis that's made you feel this distressed before.

The therapist might also want to find out how you coped in past crises. Did you suffer in silence, growing more rigid and frightened, but not letting on? Did you try to escape through some sort of chemical dependency (i.e., drugs or drink) or by spending every waking moment working until the tautness of your nerves began to fray? Did you look for help from someone who couldn't or wouldn't give it to you or even say, "Hey, let's go to the local crisis center; I think they can help you more than I can, but I'll go there with you and stay if you want me to?" How much were you able to understand in the past about *why* you were so deeply upset?

Crisis intervention, as this kind of brief therapy is called, is more than "tea and sympathy," or emotional Scotch tape. The goal, in many instances, is not just to reduce the roiling anxiety and get you back to the way you were before. It also can be the means to a better understanding of yourself and of how to handle (if not avoid) similar crises in the future without becoming totally immobilized.

Sometimes brief therapy is a terrific help in non-crisis situations. Just a few sessions can put a whole new complexion on something that's been stalking you for a long time—some quirk about only liking boys who treat you badly, or maybe a problem with getting up the nerve to assert yourself even when you know you're right. Maybe it's a family situation—or the aftereffects of one; a general bleakness or a sense of futility about your future or right now. Getting at the source of these problems may not be as difficult or as grueling as you think.

Take Ginny, for example. She was constantly criticized and bossed at home; her parents were always comparing her unfavorably to her older sisters. For the past year, Ginny has been shoplifting regularly "just for kicks." After getting caught twice in one store, Ginny agreed to see a therapist "to keep everyone happy." Personally, she thought it was silly.

The therapist she went to began in an unpushy way, listening soberly as she explained why she had come ("It was coming here or going to court.") Then he said, well, as long as you *are* here and the time is paid for and all that, is there anything you would care to talk about?

Ginny didn't answer; she just shrugged.

"No problems?"

"None."

"Fantastic! You must have an unusually good situation. What are your parents like?"

"Well," Ginny sighed, "as a matter of fact, they stink on ice! They're cold and mean and nothing I can do ever pleases them. They do nothing but criticize me; they can't stand any boy I go out with, they don't like the way I look. My marks at school are never good enough no matter how hard I try. They're sore as hell that I'm not another little genius like my sisters." Ginny began to talk more freely, admitting how anxious for approval she was—and had been for as long as she could remember—how very hurt she was that her parents seemed to be dissatisfied with everything about her. "Can I come back?" she asked the therapist eagerly when the hour was up.

Gradually, she realized that her stealing was an attempt to get her parents' attention and concern. ("I guess I really craved it!") With the therapist, Ginny began to build a concept of who *she* was—apart from her parents' or anyone else's opinion of her. In just four sessions, Ginny had begun to do some important reevaluation.

Whether it's a couple of sessions or a dozen or more, therapy can be quite an adventure, peeling away all the stuff that isn't you and dusting off what is. Dr. Thomas McGinnis, psychologist and author of *Open Family Living,* looks at it that way. When a new person comes in and seems ill at ease and anxious about what's going to happen, Dr. McGinnis explains to the person, "Whoever you are makes sense. I want to listen to you, and I'll try to give you reliable and valid feedback, and we'll both be learning about how you got to be you. . . . If that sounds like a drag, I'll show you what an exciting person you are: you're thinking and feeling all the time! The dullness is just an outside thing . . . I want to help you develop skills for getting in touch with yourself and communicating that intouchness to others and for helping others to do the same with you."

Getting from here to there: its ups and downs

The good feelings and improvements may not always appear immediately—or continuously. It's no picnic to poke and probe at the stuff you have neatly avoided in the past; and as those sources of conflict become more accessible to you, it's not unusual to feel a little worse *on the way* to feeling substantially better.

Sometimes, as much as we may *want* to get in touch with ourselves, we start out very rigidly, with a chip on the shoulder. The following is a not-uncommon scene between a young person and a therapist:

Young Person: "Well, I really just came here to prove I'm not crazy."

Therapist: "I'll write letters to the world, if that's all you want; really, if you were crazy, you wouldn't have thought of coming here. Like all of us, you have scar tissue . . . you may not be interested in working . . . okay, if not, fine. But I suggest you come in a couple of times and try it out. I'll try not to let *my* problems contaminate you anymore than I can help . . . I'll be working on me just as I'm working on you. . . ."

Young Person: "That's a little patronizing."

Therapist: "Well, good. You just shared a feeling, a momentary event of your own insides. See, your feeling motor never stops! I didn't mean to be patronizing. Sure, I've worked on my problems a good deal, but I want to work hard and do the very best I can for you. We're going to work according to what you tell me you want, where *you* want to go."

And so it might begin.

Whether or not you walk into a therapy situation free of any trepidations, there still are bound to be some ups and downs. Gaining awareness and control of the hang-ups that have been running your show is not just a goal, but a process. It implies growing and changing, and *that* means giving up old, established, and peculiarly comfortable ways of trying to cope. Believe it or not, it's entirely possible to feel nostalgic about your old defenses against the bad feelings, even when you know better than anyone else how manifestly lousy, ineffectual, and self-defeating they have been.

As much as a person in therapy wants to progress and achieve certain liberating goals, some small part of him wants to cling to the old suffering. This "resistance," as it is called, may not make too much sense, but it is terribly human. Here are some of the ways in which it can show up.

Diversionary tactics. This may mean glossing over what's really bothering you and harping—at great length—on what sounds juicy but isn't. (This subterfuge is designed to make the therapist think you're being cooperative and earnest when in fact you're carefully revealing nothing.)

Growing sullen, arriving late, "forgetting" appointments. You can either be obvious about the fact that you've decided to quit cooperating, or devious (a variation is coming in all bright and cheery one day and announcing that you quite suddenly feel super, terrific, all better, and goodbye-thanksverymuch).

Trying to rationalize the problem away. Using

your wits to outfox the shrink (and you) is the name of this game. You do it by *defending* your problems instead of scrutinizing them for clues to what is causing them or searching for alternative ways of behaving.

Miscellaneous. There are more devious and inventive ways of resisting, some too subtle for either patient or therapist to spot right off. Certainly resistance is no reason for feeling guilty or deciding that you're "failing." It is inconvenient in the sense that it bogs you down; however, it can be taken as a sign of real progress! The very fact that you're consciously or unconsciously saying "whoa!" and sweating a bit suggests that you're hitting paydirt, getting closer to those conflicts-under-cover that have been causing you problems.

Sometimes the resistance is a reflection of the fact that you've let yourself trust the therapist more than you had ever intended to (and maybe more than you have allowed yourself to trust any other adult including your parents). But this time, for some reason, you've refrained from mobilizing the usual prickly pear defenses, and so here you are—trusting the guy. You do a quick double take and think "let me out of here!"

One of the therapist's hardest jobs is to be sensitive to the various forms resistance can take—*and* to what might be lurking behind it in each instance. He can't know all the ways, especially when you're good at it. If you want to get somewhere instead of just marking time, it's your job to be vigilant of your sly and sometimes inadvertent attempts to sabotage your own progress.

In other words, knowing you're resisting and letting yourself continue to fool the therapist is just cutting off your nose to spite your face. However, recognizing that you are resisting and *telling* the therapist what you think you might be up to is very productive and very mature.

In fact, when properly "dissected" and examined, that subtle (or not so subtle) foot-dragging routine of yours can actually lead to deeper understanding and quicker results for you than if you'd never gotten to the point of feeling as if you had to put up roadblocks.

Does understanding always *have to* precede *those desired changes?*

Not according to the advocates of a school of therapy known as behavior-change. Just as you can debate whether the chicken or the egg came first, so can you argue whether you have to understand a problem before you can correct it or whether you can attack it directly without a lot of introspection.

There are plenty of people who want to make changes in their personalities but don't want to bother making an exhaustive search through their psyches for the "key" to their behavior. This is especially true if it is something very specific and tangible they want to accomplish—like getting over a fear of dogs, giving up smoking, or getting over feeling unreasonably guilty and responsible for a parental divorce.

In behavior-change, or behavior modification therapy, the changes are made first, and then, it is hoped, the anxiety will go away. This is the opposite of trying to first ease the anxiety in the hope that the desired changes in behavior will follow. Some therapists say that behavior-change can be at least as useful and definitely faster than the other kind of therapy—especially in combating habits and fears that we wish we didn't have.

What happens in behavior-change therapy is this. The therapist helps the patient develop a planned program of deliberate actions and ways of thinking which are designed to short-circuit the self-defeating old ways of perceiving and responding to situations, and to substitute and reinforce new, better ways.

If you think it sounds a little like a trained seal act—or those lab mice going through their paces—you are right, insofar as behavior-change therapy did develop out of the study of animal behavior. (If mice can be trained to act in certain ways by giving them rewards—or punishment—according to whether you want them to repeat or quit the thing they're doing at that moment, why not humans?)

In therapy, however, you are far from a helpless rodent; after all, you're the one who's come in asking for help in making those specific alterations. Nothing is being done to you or without your say-so.

If, for example, you have a tendency to avoid social situations because you feel shy and foolish and inferior, the therapist might suggest a certain "behavioral prescription" for you; *he* may formulate it, but it still takes *your* determined effort to follow the relearning plan in an active and conscientious way.

If you are like Cece, a girl who falls in love on the first meeting with virtually every guy only to end up despising him a few weeks later, your "homework" might consist of following the therapist's suggestion that you continue to see one fellow (even if you can't stand him anymore) instead of casting him aside. Then you can see for yourself that the boy is human and neither the model of perfection you first imagined him to be nor the crumb he was inevitably slated to become in your eyes. In your therapy sessions, you would be able to discuss your feelings and reactions to the anxieties which your new behavior is bringing to the surface.

Does this approach sound good to you? Some therapists swear by it (or some modified form of it); others find it too facile and liable to backfire. There is the story of the woman who went to a behavior-change therapist to be cured of her drinking. The therapist was not about to trifle with helping her try to figure out what was making her withdraw into an alcoholic haze; his bag was to attack her habit of thinking of liquor as something helpful or fun or relaxing. What he did was, he had her take a drink of gin immediately followed by something that would make her vomit until she ached. She was supposed to repeat the process several more times. In a short while, she felt her gorge rise every time she got the merest whiff of liquor. Finally, she not only turned into a teetotaler, but whenever she was in a crowded bus or store and smelled liquor on someone's breath, she would throw up. In this woman's case, at least, the mechanical approach worked *too* well and backfired.

Even in less dramatic cases, there is always the possibility that some new symptom (possibly even more distressing than the original one) will pop out because the original problem hasn't been solved, only stifled and driven further underground. Therapy doesn't mean that you have to rehash every event in your childhood or remember all your dreams, but a little searching and some thinking and probing on your part can be an enlightening supplement to behavior-change therapy.

Which type of therapy should you choose?
It is sensitive and skilled *individuals* who bring about success in therapy, not any magical methods or foolproof formulas. Sure, some people are very gung ho about one "school" of therapy or another, but it has been scientifically shown over and over that there is just no clear-cut evidence that any one type of therapy is superior to another.

Some friend may swear that "primal scream therapy" or "Adlerian" or "Sullivanian" is *the* "only kind" of therapy, and it has made her a new person. Great! But it still doesn't mean that it's the right thing for you. Earth shoes, wedges, or six-inch heels may be all the rage and terrifically comfortable for someone else, but what matters is which shoes feel right on *your* feet.

Many therapists reject the idea of identifying which "brand" of therapy they practice. Each therapist is more than just a product of the views of a certain training institute or teacher. Your therapist is an individual with his or her own carefully synthesized technique, style, and way of working.

We know of one therapist who makes a point of adjusting his style ("a balance of thinking, feeling, and acting") to fit the needs of the individual patient. "For example," he explains, "if someone is too intellectual in his life at the expense of feeling, I might use one kind of approach; or if he's flooded with feeling, feeling all over the place and acting like he doesn't have a brain in his head, I'd do something different." It is how you get along, whether you feel like you can trust the therapist, and whether you have the sense that he or she is smart and sensitive enough to help you accomplish something that should determine your choice of a therapist. If the shoe fits, wear it, and if not, don't let it chafe or pinch—keep shopping around!

5

Therapy in a group: the pros and cons

Therapy isn't always a one-to-one arrangement. Individual therapy has no monopoly on getting results; in fact, one therapist states emphatically that "anything powerful that can happen in individual therapy can happen in a group."

The major difference between group therapy and individual therapy is obvious—there are others in there with you! Group therapy is different from a classroom situation, a party, a club meeting, or a gathering of strangers waiting for a bus in that you are all in therapy to explore each other's emotional life and conflicts, and to work on problems together.

The group members (who may or may not be in individual therapy as well) might share a common problem, such as having to cope with the ravaging effects of living with a drug-addicted parent. Or the group members might have been handpicked by the therapist in order to get a balance of different personality types or a blend of different strengths and weaknesses.

Some innovative groups have been formed—groups of couples with marital problems, for instance. Certain therapists are working with groups composed of teenagers and other teenagers' parents, as opposed to their own (for some people, this is a less threatening, less emotionally charged situation).

In any case, unlike encounter groups, which are usually conducted more in the spirit of ships-passing-in-the-night, group therapy is an ongoing affair, rather than a one-or-two-shot deal. The people in the group may have started out as strangers, but they usually develop a teamlike feeling and a mutually concerned and helpful attitude. This atmosphere seems to pretty much wipe out any sense of embarrassment or fear of being laughed at or gossiped about that a member might initially feel.

Groups are not for everyone

No, they are not . . . and especially not for the thin-skinned or the super-shy. Group members tend to be more outspoken and blunt than a therapist. And, of course, not all of the critical things they say are going to be fair, accurate, or clearly distinguished from their own hang-ups. In other words, group therapy might—especially at first—be tough for someone who is easily hurt. (With individual therapy, you can at least be certain that your words *won't* be falling on potentially negative, arrogant, or inattentive ears.)

Another potential drawback to group therapy lies in the fact that in a group you may have to compete for attention. (After all, you came here to solve *your* problems, not Bob's or Carol's or Ted's or Alice's or Henry's, and they didn't even get to you today.) This can make it kind of a strain, especially if you are very agitated about something or if you're the type who needs time to relax and open up. But before you get fully into the mood, someone in the group is interrupting you to talk about a problem that *he* just remembered. So, if you feel that you need the privacy, the quiet understanding, and the unpressured pace of one-to-one therapy, the group may not be the best form for you.

There are advantages

Yes! Quite beyond the fact that group therapy is usually less expensive, it is absolutely false to think that groups are second-rate or not as good as individual therapy. In fact, there are some distinct advantages to group therapy.

• A cast of characters. Group members can relate to each other in various ways, pointing up problem areas that might not emerge as clearly if it's just the person and the therapist.

• Safety in numbers. The presence of others can

take some pressure off one individual, particularly if you feel threatened by the therapist. (In a group, someone *else* can talk now and then, and give you a breather.)

• Extra feedback. It's nice to have the affirmation, the criticism, and the multiple moment-to-moment reactions of a group of your own peers sometimes, rather than just the comments of the therapist. Whether he does or doesn't actually live in his own little world, it can *seem* that way to some people; and, consequently, they're skeptical of even the encouraging, congratulatory things their therapists might say. In a group, on the other hand, "it's even okay when the whole group seems to be attacking you," one young woman marveled. "It convinces you that they're taking you and all your problems seriously; that you matter—and that they think you are capable of doing better. It is very encouraging, it buoys you up and makes you want to work."

Doing it in the family way

Family therapy is becoming more and more common these days. It differs both from individual and group therapy because its emphasis is on not a random or hand-selected group, but on a family group. The purpose of family therapy is to cool the tensions and work on improving the troublesome and troubled relationships found within the family.

Here are some of the kinds of things that might be part of the deal:

• *Getting conflicts out in the open where they can be scrutinized and dealt with.* For instance, why does everyone in the X family get mad at Dorothy? What's the source of brother Jim's power over the parents? And how does each person in the family really feel about the obviously unequal treatment Dorothy and Jim are receiving from their parents?

• *Getting the family to acknowledge what is really going on.* Why do they all let Jim dominate them with his temper? Are the parents unable or unwilling to assert themselves? What illusions might Jim's stormy tantrums be helping them to maintain—about him and about themselves? Are they using him to punish themselves? For what? Why the kid-gloves approach? How did Dorothy get cast in the scapegoat role? Does her Cinderella position in the family really stem from *her* actions as her parents have claimed, or could it be the outcrop of a whole network of displaced needs on the part of the parents?

• *Improving communications.* This is simply the underrated art of learning to talk to one another—and to listen—instead of the usual icy silences or nagging, yelling bouts.

• *Getting the family interested in treating each*

other more respectfully, more lovingly. Even beyond—or before—tackling the serious problems, family therapy can help family members learn to spot
—in advance—those little ways everyone in the family seems to have of hurting one another just to "get
even." Breaking that pattern of automatic putdowns can be a big relief and can pave the way for
improving and strengthening relationships.

What's special about family therapy?

Again, it isn't just treatment *in* a group, it's treatment *for* a group. That group is a pre-existing one
that continues to be a group twenty-four hours a
day, seven days a week.

Members of a family group in therapy are very
much involved with one another, and, consequently,
even less likely to be objective about one another's
problems than the members of a group of mere
acquaintances would be.

Some family therapists work in a straightforward
way; others are more inclined to disturb the peace,
deliberately. A therapist might, for example, ask
each member of the family to explain one another's
behavior. Or a different therapist might have the
family use psychodrama (role-playing) to really
get into each other's heads, to *feel* what the other
is feeling. The therapist might goad a son or daugh-
ter to come out and ask a troubling question of a

parent . . . or make a heartfelt request that he or she hadn't ever felt could be verbalized before.

There are some family therapists who use non-verbal communication as a way of getting things going. There is one therapist who asks family members to touch each other, move around the room, sprawl on the floor, and make faces at one another, in the hope that something unexpected will happen to undo the old, predictable patterns and wake people up.

Hearing about this kind of emotionally charged therapy, a lot of people would probably wonder if it isn't scary or dangerous to leave a session with all those raw emotions exposed. The answer is that a responsible therapist will not leave things hanging unresolved, but will see to it that the family leaves the session feeling better than when they came in, because the air has been cleared and the work has been constructive.

Some family therapists work on the theory that there are no troubled people, only troubled families. But not all the therapists who treat family members together are so gung ho for the form. They'll do it for certain clients, but will still treat most of the people who come to them on a strictly individual basis. Dr. Selma Miller, President of the New York Association of Marriage and Family Counselors, feels that for family therapy to be of any real use, the whole family has to be willing to work and co-operate. Here is an example:

Paul, the son of a millionaire

Paul was a bright fifteen-year-old who would have been reasonably handsome and athletic if it hadn't been for the fact that he was some 80 to 100 pounds overweight.

"He's got a serious health problem, a risk to his heart," the family doctor had said. He put Paul on a diet, which only made Paul gain an extra five pounds. The family doctor scratched his head and gave Paul's mother the name and phone number of a family therapist in the next town.

"We'd been bothered about Paul's weight for a long time, but we just didn't want to get on his back," Paul's mother said when she called to make the appointment. "It's a relief to be finally doing something about it."

The therapist assured the family that even though the problem was quite visibly Paul's, the parents' concern and wish to help *could* be quite an asset in the therapy itself.

When the family arrived—all three well-dressed—Paul and his mother sat on a sofa in the office; the father, who seemed to have just come along for the ride, sat quite apart from them in a chair against the wall. He didn't have much to say.

Paul was polite and seemed eager to cooperate,

but he was very tentative, hesitant to speak, and very solicitous of his mother, frequently glancing at her for approval.

"I guess we're here because I'm too fat," Paul said, watching his mother's face. Paul's mother took over then and went into a long description of Paul's various unsuccessful attempts to quit snacking between meals.

The therapist said that he would like to make a videotape of the session and then play it back for the family so that they could all observe and discuss it together. The family agreed—and the results were very revealing. Here's what came out:

Every time Paul started to say something, his mother would smile gently at him and rephrase whatever he said. The mother was horrified when she saw the videotape to discover how much she talked, how she never looked at her husband. Paul noticed with a bitter little laugh that his father was "almost out of the picture," sitting so far away from the others.

Paul's father cleared his throat and said that he had nothing to add, at which point Paul blurted out, "That's just the trouble, you never do." It was the first time he had gotten angry at his father in years— or even admitted to himself that he was mad at him.

In subsequent sessions, Paul noticed that he always seemed to turn to his mother. The therapist asked if he remembered why, or if he noticed himself doing it at home. The whole family acknowledged that they did not have the best relationship with one another. The mother felt that perhaps she was trying to use Paul for the companionship her husband was not providing.

Paul began to see how he had been stuffing himself in order to deny his anger at his mother for imposing herself on him, and his anger at his father for his passivity.

Gradually, Paul began to see the positive side of his father, a successful, self-made man with an enviable reputation in the business world. Paul began to seek out his father's advice in making certain decisions about elective courses and chess club activities at school.

"Things were a bit raw for a while," the therapist observed. "Tears were shed and bitter words spoken; but this was a family willing to say 'I want to change' rather than 'do something to change him' or 'make her different.'"

Even if the family situation seems to be at the root of someone's trouble, it still may not always help to treat the family together; in other words, as the following example shows, it is not always true that a family can—or should—be involved in the young person's therapy.

Doris, a babe in the woods

Doris, seventeen, was a quiet, pretty teenager whose father had died when she was seven and whose mother was overprotective to the point that Doris had no life of her own. (For one thing, her mother would pick her up at school every day so that Doris would not have to walk through a "questionable" neighborhood on her way to the public bus—along with hundreds of other students.)

The summer before her senior year in high school, Doris begged and cajoled her mother into letting her take a waitressing job at a resort. Doris, up to that point, had been so restricted in her activities that she had had few friends, no dates, and no social or sexual experiences whatever. Consequently, when Russell, the lifeguard, made a big play for Doris, she was so innocent and so flattered that he had her in bed with him in no time.

Doris took it for granted that Russell was madly in love with her and that they were as good as engaged; when she found out otherwise, she was shocked and hurt and told her mother (who phoned every night). Her mother became furious, yelled at Doris, called her names, and made her come back home.

Doris was feeling confused and hurt and very, very guilty. Her mother, still angry and deeply concerned, sent Doris to a therapist. It worked out well. Doris went to five or six sessions by herself, and that brief therapy succeeded in helping Doris to climb out from under the heavy load of guilt she felt about her affair with Russell.

Then, when it became apparent to the therapist

that Doris' major problem was in handling her well-meaning but stranglingly overprotective and bossy mother, the therapist agreed to Doris' own request that the mother come along too for some family therapy.

Doris' mother was only too happy to come; but it was not, the therapist observed, because she was open to making changes in her own attitudes and behavior. Doris' mother only wanted to get in on the act and regain the control that Doris had already begun to slip out of.

In the first joint session, the mother did everything she could to undermine the therapist, to "prove" that Doris was immature and unreasonable and very much in need of her mother's "protection."

"I could see Doris looking at me," the therapist said, "as if to say, 'Oh, come on, are you going to let her do this to *you* too?'" Neither that session nor the three or four that followed made so much as a nick in Doris' mother's determination to control Doris.

Doris was crushed. She had expected the therapist to "make" her mother change. But instead her mother was now totally against the therapist, calling her a fraud and saying that she wasn't going to pay for Doris to go anymore.

Doris, however, continued to go to the therapist at a reduced fee of $1.00 per session, paid for out of her summer earnings. Gradually, then, Doris was able to develop the fortitude to cope with her mother. She learned to not just automatically obey nor mindlessly defy her mother's authority, but to make her own judgments (even if some would be wrong). She learned to get home from school by herself, without coddling *or* any unnecessary, crazy risks. All of these actions helped open the door for Doris to get to know and spend time with girls and boys. Doris' situation improved, the therapist said, but in this case it was in spite of the fact that her mother had come into the act, not because of it.

Couples counseling

This is yet another kind of help you can get, and it's something you might want to consider if your boyfriend or girlfriend is as much of a problem as a job, or if your relationship has hit some major snag. It can—but doesn't have to—be a deep-digging kind of thing. It can, in any case, be a great help in alerting you to the real issues behind that recurring tiff or those doubts that keep nagging.

Marriage counseling *per se* is not new. Even premarital counseling is well known. (Since 1970, in fact, it's been mandatory in California for young couples of which one partner is under eighteen to receive this kind of counseling as a condition for the court to grant permission to marry.)

But the thing that surprises a lot of people is that you don't have to be married or engaged—or of any particular age—to be eligible for this help.

Here are some examples of typical problems and how a couples' counselor might approach them:

• *Sue and Ted have been going together—unhappily for two years. They continually try to break up but always go back together.* The counselor would ask pertinent questions to help each of them to understand what they are really giving each other and why they are clinging to an unfulfilling relationship. (Are they afraid to be unattached? Are they straining the relationship by trying to make it do double-duty as an escape from parental and school pressures?) The counselor would *not* presume to tell Sue and Ted not to see each other, nor would he try to persuade them to try to make a go of it after all.

• *Ann and Ronald are always fighting about Ronald's drag racing. Ann hates it and Ronald refuses to quit. They love each other.* First, the counselor would try to make sure that the racing issue is an isolated one in an otherwise harmonious relationship. Then, instead of imposing his values on the couple or lecturing either of them, he would try to get them to accept one another's point of view and arrive at a compromise. This could be having Ronald limit his races to one or two nights a week and going without Ann, or having Ann go with him but not criticize him, *nor* be pressured to participate.

• *Patty and Frank are at odds over how exclusive their relationship should be: she wants him all to herself; he claims he loves her but wants to date others.* The counselor, in all likelihood, would try to help Patty to understand that Frank isn't willing to make a commitment to her and that trying to tie him down wouldn't get them anywhere. He would *not* try to persuade Frank to stop fooling around, but he would help Patty examine her real motives in clinging and explore the various options that she *does* have—such as breaking up with Frank or staying together and dating others too, or dating only Frank but understanding that he may never "come around."

• *Kate and George are upset over her parents' disapproval of him. It's even beginning to show up in their schoolwork.* The counselor would probably *not* call up Kate's parents—either to scold or plead with them. He would tell Kate and George that it's natural to be upset by parental disapproval—especially when you're still living at home. He would try to help them get in touch with their *own* feelings about each other, as separate from those of parents, friends, or any other outside people.

"There is no lecturing, no absolute right or wrong and few direct answers in couples' counseling," says Dr. Miller. "The purpose of it is to explore the partners' needs—and whether they are serving those needs in the best way that they can."

6
Without any hassle

Good for you!
It's great that there are so many more therapists
and counselors around and available than there
ever used to be: not only in terms of numbers, but
also geographically. This is all to the good, but as
far as young people are concerned, what's been
even more of a boon is the whole new *accessibility*
of help.

Ever since the 1960s, when the drug-and-hippie-
culture took over and so many people were strung
out and lost and it was apparent that traditional
sources of help weren't very good at dealing with
these situations, the mental health people and
agencies *have* been scurrying to update and expand
and rethink their services and their whole approach
to young people. They have taken many steps to
make therapy less intimidating and more palatable—

and it's something all but the stodgiest therapists are continuing to strive for.

For the most part, the traditional services did *not* invent this more loosened-up and acceptable help for young people. What these agencies have been doing is trying to emulate some of the flexibility and dynamic enthusiasm of the various drop-in centers, youth service bureaus, runaway houses, and other programs geared especially to the young and to those who either reject (or feel rejected by) the kinds of services already around.

The best of these newer, teen-oriented programs have made a huge impact, in part because (1) they provide a rigorously screened, high-quality and dedicated professional staff, and (2) they have done such an excellent job of clearing the major kinds of obstacles young people have faced in the past in search of counseling.

Here are some of the barriers that have been eased:

• *Overcoming legal hassles.* What if the only therapist or agency in your area has refused to treat (or even *see*) you without your parents' consent? An awful lot of people would have to just say "forget it!" It is less likely to happen now, because, even in states where the laws are still less than sympathetic to the needs of a teenager who has to talk to someone right away but can't (or doesn't want to) get his parents in on it, the newer type of counseling center will not turn a young person away, and will guarantee him a chance to talk to someone there.

• *Overcoming financial hassles.* One of the reasons therapists and clinics need that parental consent for treating a minor is that they like to know that someone is willing to foot the bill. Traditional agencies have always been willing to offer free services *if* you happen to come from a very poor family and can prove it. But what if your family's not poor, and you need to talk to someone before you sit down with your parents and explain that you need help and why?

The newer clinics have launched the policy of not charging a fee, at least not for the initial consultation. Instead, they recruit volunteer professional therapists, and student volunteers to do the clerical work, and/or they depend on grants and private contributions.

If it appears that you want therapy and they have someone in mind for you who happens to charge a fee, that could turn out okay. Maybe by the time you have to pay, things will have simmered down at home to the point where you *can* talk to your parents and explain what you're after.

• *Credibility.* "Professional help is like Jell-O," says Dr. Michael Baizerman of the University of Minnesota's Center for Youth Development and Research. "It doesn't change in essence, but it does take on the shape of its surroundings." The newer agencies have shown the importance of making their services, their accessibility, and their trustworthiness *known* to young people in the area. It may be through ads and write-ups in the local underground paper, through good contacts with the local hotline and/or peer counselors. Maybe it's locating themselves in high-visibility, unintimidating spots like a storefront or an old house in a rundown or hippie neighborhood.

Keeping their word on matters of confidentiality and giving exactly what they promise to give is precisely why the good agencies have managed to establish—and maintain—a good, trustworthy reputation.

Not only good—but inviting!

A prime example of this type of agency is the Counseling Center of Milwaukee, Wisconsin.

"Simply offering counseling help isn't enough," the directors say. "It must be offered in a context which meets the counselee's minimum needs to the point that the individual will walk in the door."

Here are some special features of the Counseling Center:

• *First names only*. You aren't even asked for your last name when you come in there. This is why you can be absolutely certain that your parents (or the police) aren't going to be waiting outside the door at the end of your little chat. Of course, if you want to give your full name and/or bring your parents in, that is fine.

• *No red tape.* If you've gotten working papers or been to a motor vehicle office lately, you know what a drag it is to wait in a line so long and slow moving that you think the guy at the window may have left a day or so ago! Fill out this form. Start at the beginning. If you make a mistake, you lose your place.

When you've got a problem to talk about, you're even *less* in the mood for any of that bureaucratic mouse-maze. At the Counseling Center, they process a short questionnaire for you—in less than one minute! And they do it at the end rather than the beginning of the session.

• *A first session "that accomplishes something."* If the counselee doesn't feel that something has happened in the first session, he's not likely to be back for a second one. *That's* what the directors of the center have found.

To illustrate, they give the example of Joanne, a young drug abuser, who, typically, had made several "false starts" towards counseling before actually getting herself into the Counseling Center.

Joanne, a girl with many problems, had been doing downers. Those pills had, for some time, been producing a pleasant haze for her, masking out all the anxiety that she felt about her home life, her boyfriend, and the many problems she was having at school.

Joanne's decision to seek counseling was a "make it or break it" event. "Had she not been seen fairly quickly or had she been told to make an appointment and come back then, her first session might never have happened. It did happen though, and a lot happened in it." Even though Joanne had no appointment, she was seen within twenty minutes. Her counselor escorted her to a small room, introducing herself merely as "Pam."

"As soon as they sat down, Pam asked Joanne why she'd come in—there were no questions about her age, her socio-economic status, or any other identifying information. Joanne had had no real idea of what to expect and the simple question cut right through the strong demeanor she was trying to present. She burst into tears. She talked for fifteen tear-filled minutes, with Pam interjecting occasional questions. The story of the most miserable month Joanne had ever spent unfolded.

"Before the session was half over, Joanne realized that someone was listening, that Pam was hearing not only her words, but also her desperation. She wasn't asking voyeuristic questions about Joanne's sex life or drug use; she asked questions about Joanne's fears, the grounds for those fears, and about the basis for Joanne's decisions over the past month. Pam listened carefully to what Joanne said, and when she commented, she asked for Joanne's *reactions* to each suggestion, to make sure that Joanne didn't feel that she was trying to dominate or push."

As it happened, Joanne did go on to take Pam's suggestion and referral, first for some family counseling (which showed Joanne that her parents cared about her much more than she had realized), and then for joining a therapy group where she could talk over her hopes and fears and thoughts with others on a regular, weekly basis.

More innovation. Counseling "to go." A special kind of help around for street people, runaways, wanderers

It is not widely known, but there *are* counselors who work, not in any office (no matter how informal), but out in the street and other public places: on a park bench, in a bus station's scarred and dreary waiting room, aboard a special roving medical van, or sitting over a cup of coffee at an all-night cafeteria—anywhere, in fact, where there might be kids who need help but don't know how to get it.

In some situations, the individual clients are referred by the courts to a youth-worker agency, in the hope that several talking sessions with the counselor—and perhaps some related group or family counseling—will help to get the kid in touch with his feelings and his options while he still has options. This help can be a way of nipping a beginning crime career or growing drug-dependency in the bud.

Sometimes an entire gang becomes the "client"—such as when a certain youth organization decides to assign a streetwork counselor to spend a lot of time building rapport with the gang members, with an aim not of busting them up but of helping them direct their group strength into something more constructive than bopping other people on the head.

Not all street counselors receive any official referrals. In fact, they often are just "out there," finding the people who seem to need them. It takes a lot of sensitivity and tact to deal with these kids, and it's especially tough if the potential client is, say, a defiant "hurry-up-and-gratify-me" kid from the suburbs with illusions of proving how grown-up he is and pretty much oblivious to the very real dangers of the streets. Nor is it any easier to win the trust of a streetwise fourteen-year-old who feels "just fine" because she's got a tough pimp to take care of her (and doesn't realize that there are alternatives).

In reaching kids like these, Bridge Over Troubled Waters, a Boston streetwork program, has been remarkably successful. For one thing, they avoid any hint of authority in the help they offer; as a result, they are known—by word of mouth—to be trustworthy, friendly, and nonjudgmental.

"On the streets where people hang out we try to reach and touch them," says Bridge director Barbara Whelan. "Our guiding principle is communicating a sense of self-respect, looking at where people are, accepting it, and stimulating them to move in their positive life directions."

Some of the Bridge workers make their rounds on foot. In addition, they operate a fully equipped and professionally-staffed "medical van" which can be found regularly in Boston, Harvard Square, and other places where young people congregate.

"Sometimes," says Ms. Whelan, "a kid will come into the van and say, 'I have a cold.' Then, a moment later, 'I've run away from home and I'm scared.'" What can Bridge offer? A number of alternatives! They are supportive, but they will not take over or urge any one particular course of action or "solution." Whether the client comes into the van or whether a counselor has spotted *him* and made the first move, nothing is done "to" the client or behind his back. The Bridge counselor can suggest temporary lodging with a volunteer family in the area or help in achieving a reconciliation with the parents. Depending on the situation, the best help might be the name of a lawyer, some leads on possible jobs, and the phone number of a problem pregnancy counseling center; or the best help might be just having a good chance to talk, eating a sandwich, and making a phone call to Traveler's Aid for help in getting home.

It's not that the counselors are cavalier about the dangers of life in the streets—on the contrary! They know very well that it is grim and frequently terrifying for these teens. The obvious health hazards like drugs, pneumonia, venereal disease, and even malnutrition almost pale before the human hazards—rapists, muggers, sadists, and predatory pimps. Still, the counselors never try to coerce anyone, because simply hauling a kid home—or even getting him "safely" off the streets against his will—accomplishes little and would only be an added incentive to his rebelling and taking off again.

Even when a young person's immediate crisis is over, Bridge is there to offer counseling help and special activities designed to promote self-awareness and self-respect. One Bridge counselor is working with a group of ex-runaways (now back at home) making a film on the streets, a project in which they are carefully analyzing their own experiences, feelings, and behavior. Another Bridge counselor managed to bring together a number of young mothers she had met individually at random on the street. Now the young women meet regularly with the counselor. They find it a warm and useful thing in their lives. Other Bridge outreach workers run basketball and swimming classes, as an alternative to "hanging" on the streets. In this way, Bridge Over Troubled Waters (and other programs dealing with runaways) is able to help their young clients deal with feelings as well as tactical problems.

The Runaway Houses: a nationwide phenomenon
Fortunately, not *all* of the estimated 1.3 to 2.1

million American kids who run away each year take
to the streets. Little by little, the word is getting out
that there are places to go when you can't stand it
at home anymore. Even if you're only *contemplating*
running, you can get immediate help from the staff
at any of a wide network of twenty-four-hour-a-day
runaway centers.

Like Bridge's street counselors, the people working at runaway houses recognize that running away
is usually not the problem *per se*, but a young person's attempt at solving whatever's been making his
life intolerable at home. Whether you finally run
because you've been physically or psychologically
abused, or because of a parent's alcoholism or bossi-
ness, or because the parent actually threw you out
and told you not to darken the doorstep again, runaway house staffers are aware of the kinds of pain
and confusion that might make you strap on your
backpack and close the front door behind you.

Besides providing emergency housing, the runaway houses offer counseling right away. Somebody
is there to listen and care. Also, many of the centers
invite young people and their parents to continue
to come for counseling even after they've gotten
together again.

More than just providing a sanctuary, what they
try to do is to help the runaway face his real feelings—including all the complicated love-hate things
about his family. They also try to get the young
person and his parents talking to one another and,

when possible, to reunite the families once the air has been cleared. Sometimes a family doesn't care about the young person who has run away, or else the parents are too abusive for the person to go back to. In cases like that, the runaway house counselor would help the young person weigh the options that he *does* have in searching for a long-range solution.

One fine runaway house—typical perhaps of many good ones coast-to-coast—is Huckleberry House in Columbus, Ohio. What Huckleberry House is all about might best be expressed in what someone has written on a wall in there: "I need you today, not tomorrow." Mike and Kathy are two of the many young people who know just what that means.

Mike

For a long time—maybe the whole two years since his mother's death—Mike had been unable to talk to his father. All he got from his dad was sarcasm and belittling. Mike also had problems at school. He felt no rapport whatsoever with any of the other students. They all seemed to be jocks or "heavy into drugs." Mike was neither. He desperately wanted to quit and go to a private technical school where he could learn computer science. He had tried to discuss this with his father, but the father just sneered and said forget it, without explaining why.

Out of sheer frustration and loneliness, Mike ran away to Huckleberry House. What he found there was a counselor he could talk to easily and openly. He shared all the bitterness he felt about his father's obvious disdain for him, his feelings of hopeless ineptitude in his few feeble attempts to make friends, and his unhappiness at not being able to share with anyone how much he missed his mother.

Mike decided to ask his father to come for a family session. His father agreed, and it was a good meeting. It turned out that Mike's father *did* care about Mike and *was* willing to try to be more tolerant and more understanding. He also agreed to act more like a companion to Mike instead of avoiding or belittling him. The father was even willing to take a new look at the merits of Mike changing schools. The upshot of all this: Mike went home and switched schools. While things weren't exactly overflowing with merriment all the time at home, Mike and his father did get along better. Besides that, Mike found in Huckleberry House a continuing source of warmth and friendship.

Kathy

After an argument with her stepmother, Kathy, fourteen, ran away and wound up (after one harrowing evening on the street) at Huckleberry House. Convinced that her father and stepmother had wanted to get rid of her ("they had tried to get a psychiatrist to say I was crazy"), Kathy had become increasingly isolated and distrustful at home.

Meanwhile, her father had begun to drink heavily and her stepmother had withdrawn from everyone, which only added to the tension, widened the gap, and made Kathy feel even less loved.

In the couple of days after Kathy's arrival at Huckleberry House, she was able to benefit from some intensive crisis-counseling and to begin to clarify her own needs and the family situation. Once Kathy had begun to feel a little more comfortable, she asked for a family session. This session was both sad and fruitful—it turned out that Kathy's parents really *were* anxious to have Kathy out of their home.

While seeking an alternative home for Kathy, Huckleberry House gave her lodging for two weeks and referred her to a therapist. Even though Kathy had not imagined the rejection she felt at home, she realized that she was sufficiently bothered by it to warrant more intensive therapy than Huckleberry House itself could provide.

Kathy's wish—to move in with a family friend—was agreeable to all concerned. Huckleberry House was able to not only smooth the transition for Kathy, but also to see that things would continue to go well for her.

To find a runaway house of high quality in your area, you can dial the toll-free, hassle-free National Runaway Switchboard (800-621-4000) at any hour.

7
In matters of life and death

Of Life

To be pregnant and single is to face one of life's
most agonizing dilemmas: all too often a woman
has to make the crucial decision alone and unsup-
ported; or, if she's very young, she has the opposite
problem of having to contend with intense pressures
and conflicting advice from family, medical "authorities," and friends.

But what about the way *she* feels? It's her body,
her life, and she is the one who will live with the consequences of whatever choice she makes.

Some women can head straight for the abortion
clinic. For many young women, however, the dilemma is overwhelming; besides the obvious practical problems and the panic and all the confusion,
there are often enormous inner conflicts—felt but
not fully understood—because accidental pregnancy

is not always an accident. Lots of times it might seem like carelessness or bad luck, but unless it's the result of rape or of a contraceptive failure to work, the pregnancy *didn't* just happen. More likely, it was the work of unacknowledged needs and desires (which may or may not include a real wish to be a mother).

Social agencies across the country (including traditional as well as counterculture ones) are beginning to recognize that young women often need a special kind of counseling with the pregnancy decision. In this counseling—even while wrestling with the logistics and the practical pros and cons of a very immediate and scary problem—the idea is not to push one course of action or another. The point is to help the woman shed the stuff she thinks she "ought" to be feeling, and begin to explore what she has been feeling, what she *is* feeling, so that even beyond making the right personal decision about her pregnancy, she can gain a good deal more control over the future course of her life.

Here's the way it works.

To avoid being pushy. The counselor's attitude and basic preparation are important, whether the client is fairly sure that she does (or doesn't) want a baby or whether she's passive and terrified and longing to be told what to do. To be sure and keep his own feelings out of it, the counselor has done some personal soul-searching: How does he really feel about abortion and even about premarital sex? Are there any hidden Puritanical feelings lurking under his outwardly enlightened beliefs? This preliminary step is bound to make his approach to the client more genuine and helpful.

When the client comes in, the good counselor doesn't begin with a lecture or a pep talk. First, he may ask her what she felt about coming to see a counselor. (According to Nancy Elizabeth Rains of the super-enlightened Walk-In Counseling Center in Minneapolis, "clients who are contemplating abortion have been culturally primed to expect condemnation.")

He may also encourage the client to talk about the symptoms of her pregnancy—emotional as well as physical ones. Nan Miller, a social worker with the Youth Consultation Service, a counseling center for adolescents in White Plains, New York, says that it is helpful when the client can say whether she feels guilty or angry at herself for becoming pregnant. Is she feeling particularly dejected and alone? Have she and her boyfriend just broken up over the pregnancy?

To make it easier, the counselor will try to avoid talking about "the father of the baby," instead she will use a term that is less emotionally charged, like "partner," as Planned Parenthood staffers have suggested. There is no point in compounding the pain. The counselor also has a weather eye out for subtle signs of trouble. For example, too casual an attitude toward the whole thing may belie fear the woman isn't necessarily conscious of. According to Ms. Miller, it is "important to help the client view her pregnancy as a part of her emotional needs and not as an isolated problem which can be wiped out and forgotten."

How she got there

How did the supposedly unwanted pregnancy occur? Was it ignorance in placing too much trust in a "safe time of the month?" Was it a do-it-yourself contraceptive method that didn't turn out? Or, if the couple didn't use anything at all, why not? Exploring the possible reasons can help a woman see what she might have been up to.

• Did she feel, for example, that using a diaphragm would make her look "like a pro": too prepared, too aggressive? It may sound more romantic and demure to be "carried away by the passion of the moment"; but isn't it really more girlish than womanly to abdicate responsibility that way?

• Was she playing at being indestructible, invulnerable; the old nothing-bad-can-happen-to-me syndrome?

• Was she using the health argument, "the pill is bad for my body?" But if that were really the entire reason, then why not some other method of birth control rather than none at all?

All of this is not done with a Sherlock Holmesian "aha!"; the client is also looking for some answers. Sure, the truth *could* be a little embarrassing if it weren't for the tact and real concern of the counselor. For instance:

• Did she simply not bother using any method of birth control because "my life is already so messed up, it wouldn't even matter if something *else* happened?"

• Did she perhaps—on some deep level, at least— *want* this to happen? To "get even" with her parents? To get away from them? To make a defiant statement—and an escape—all in one?

• Did she secretly think that pregnancy would establish her identity as a grown-up woman? ("Sometimes," says Ms. Miller, "a girl has a need to be pregnant as a means of improving her self-image and worth as a productive person and as a woman.")

It can be *especially* useful to do this kind of exploration when the unwanted pregnancy is a repeat performance. Take Danielle, for example. She had an abortion when she was a freshman in high school. Now she is eighteen, working as a receptionist, and taking a film course. She lives at home and is very indecisive about career plans, moving out of the house (which she claims she "needs" to do), and so on. She admits that her second and current "care-lessness" might have sprung from a vague hope of being rescued by a man she's dated on and off for years from a childlike role at home, and made into an instant adult as wife—and mother! She realizes now that the fellow probably won't marry her and certainly doesn't love her. She is—in the back of her mind—semi-resigned to a second abortion, but she feels victimized.

Like other repeaters, Danielle is basically unable or unwilling to care for herself. Some women allow themselves to become pregnant again and again, not out of a wish to have a baby, but from a desire to be pregnant. Unconsciously, they see pregnancy as a way of feeling better about themselves: less depressed, less childike and insignificant, and more worthwhile. Other repeaters display a need and an unerring potential for being betrayed, abandoned, and "tricked."

The counselor, in helping Danielle identify her problem, would be able to help her see how this feeling can come from childhood conditioning in a home where bad treatment seems so much better than being taken for granted or ignored. It's as close to self-worth as anything she's felt. Instead of hitting Danielle with the fact that she probably "asked for it," the counselor in this case would try to get Danielle to see that it is irrational and fruitless to pursue a dream of a shortcut to adulthood, to hope for rescue from the need to take initiative in moving out or starting a career or just saying, "Hey, this is my life, and I'm the one who has to make the choices." The counselor would have to be very careful to keep from snowing Danielle—even with lots of good sense—lest she just go along with the wishes of the counselor, secretly feeling persecuted and more helpless and unlucky than ever.

Special circumstances

Sometimes getting pregnant "accidently" is a way of trying to regain lost love; sometimes the key is right within the woman's recent past. Did she secretly think it would be a way of holding on to the guy? Did someone *else* in her life disappear recently? (Ms. Miller says that "for many girls, the history includes the death of or abandonment by a parent, and unresolved feelings about the loss.")

Making the big decision

By now the woman has had a chance to look into some of her unrealistic assumptions—and the feelings that may have led her to them. The more honesty and self-awareness she's been able to muster, the better her decision will be. Now, for whatever reason *why* she got into her dilemma, she and she alone must decide what to do about it. The counselor's help must be subtle. Careful attention to the woman's own feelings and wishes, as opposed to some outside standard of "fitness," isn't just kind, it's also sensible. A young girl who gets pregnant may yield to her mother's benign insistence that she'd be better off with an abortion than a baby, only to get pregnant again in six months and say, "Okay, *this* one is for me."

Alice and her boyfriend, John, have been together for four years. They are both sophomores in college now. Their relationship has been secure and happy and they are planning to be married "someday." Alice is pregnant—and torn by a fear of abortion and of its emotional side effects, guilt, and the possibility that afterwards, she and John might come to resent each other. At the same time, she is afraid of being so tied down by a child that she would not be able to finish her studies and become a physical therapist. She is considering all possibilities—including having the baby and *not* marrying John. At least that way nobody would feel guilty, and John wouldn't feel trapped, she says.

In this case, Alice was encouraged to consider whether her career plans were really serious or whether she had just gotten into the habit of thinking she wanted to be a woman with a career. The basic question was, why did she let herself become pregnant at this time? Perhaps she really wanted to quit school and couldn't admit it after having invested so much time and effort.

In a stable relationship such as this, it is desirable to get the man in on the counseling. Ms. Miller says that in joint interview, the young woman and her boyfriend (or husband or parent) are encouraged to become aware of and express their feelings. "Each person gains a better understanding of what the other is experiencing and what an abortion entails emotionally and physically. This discussion often helps the young woman make her decision." There was always the possibility that Alice was saying she wanted an abortion because she thought (perhaps mistakenly) that abortion was what *John* wanted. Or because she was afraid of the coercion implied in a "shot-gun" wedding. And, too, there was the possibility, Alice realized, that deep down she was just a little unsure about John's affection for her and became pregnant as a way of holding onto him. *And,* it may also have been that she wanted a baby very much, and couldn't quite face the fact that she didn't want John any longer.

To deal with Alice's fear that abortion would leave her with emotional scars, the counselor stressed the fact that such side effects nowadays are self-limiting—especially with counseling and the opportunity to work it out. Along with a greater acceptance of abortion by society and the law, the counseling opportunity lessens the guilt on the part of a woman having an abortion, and also lessens her mourning for the baby that never was.

Even when she knows what she wants, the client can benefit a lot from an honest look at why she has made the choice she has made

Says Ms. Rains: "Women who view abortion as a 'magic solution' for problems beyond the stresses associated with an unwanted pregnancy should be cautioned to seek further counseling." Just because a woman has no further need to go on being pregnant once she has "gotten even" with her family, or once she's resigned to the reality that the man is still not interested in marrying her, that woman may know that she wants to terminate her pregnancy. She still could benefit from counseling, though.

Sometimes a woman is "very sure" she wants to have the baby. The counselor can be a very helpful sounding board. If the young client wants the baby badly enough (even if some of her motives seem selfish or immature), it is not the counselor's place to dissuade her from having and keeping it; no one can say that she would not be a good mother.

After a discussion of motives and consequences, the woman might realize that it's not really a baby she wants, but a twenty-year project, a new role in life, or someone to "guarantee" her some love. Another woman might arrive at the same truths but find that her deep desire for a child of her own is unaffected. Nobody wants a baby for just one reason; there are also cases where the chief motive is benign and maternal and mature (like a longing for the pleasure of watching a child grow), but it is not intense enough to support a young single mother through the hassles inherent in raising a child alone. This, too, can be brought to light during counseling.

Sometimes a woman may be very adamant and convincing about how much she wants to keep the child. She herself doesn't even realize that it's all a kind of "lesser-evil" coverup for her fear of what she sees as a fate worse than motherhood. Lee, a self-described "swinger" who isn't even sure which of her various "friends and acquaintances" she has to thank for her pregnancy, was saying how grand motherhood would be, until the counselor began to ask what kind of arrangements Lee would make for supporting and caring for the child. Lee drew a blank, began to fidget, and gradually owned up to the fact that she was scared, "terrified of the physical pain, scared an abortion will wreck my insides."

The counselor was able to reassure Lee, to explain that her misconceptions go back to all the years when abortion was illegal and shrouded in an aura of scandal, crime, sadism, and danger, when illegal abortionists often wanted to punish the women they aborted. The counselor helped Lee see that despite her denials, she may have been harboring some very normal remorse. Her fantasy of becoming sterile from a modern, safe abortion may be based in part on a feeling that sterility is logical and fitting punishment for the crime of killing a fetus. The counselor also helped Lee understand that her fear of pain is not too realistic, since abortions today are a lot less painful than childbirth. The counselor showed Lee that her fear might be masking a deeper emotional pain about the pregnancy and maybe about her life-style in general.

Afterwards . . .

There are many ways in which a counselor can help *after* the decision has been made, as well. For one thing, the counselor can see that the woman gets a personalized course in birth control—allowing for plenty of feedback. At the clinic or at a doctor's by referral, the woman must be allowed to express her fears of "dangerous chemicals" or of any other real or imaginary side effects from the pill, for example, or she may not take it faithfully when it's prescribed. Similarly with a diaphragm, if it makes her squeamish, she should be encouraged to say so. A woman must be comfortable and committed to whatever form of birth control she chooses, or she will "forget" to use it and run the risk of another unplanned pregnancy.

On the less concrete but equally important side, the counselor can either refer a client for some therapy if she wants it (sometimes it takes some crisis like an abortion to focus in on emotional problems), or, if counselor and client had a good rapport, he might offer some post-abortion counseling himself.

Says Ms. Rains: "Pregnancy termination may become part of the problem, not just the solution. At least 20 percent of the women who were followed up . . . report reservations about and depressions over their decision . . . Counselors who have done post-abortion counseling feel it takes between three and six weeks for some clients' relief to turn to remorse."

At this point, a counselor says, "it is very, very important to help a woman realize that she hurts. Most people exhaust themselves trying to fight off what they think they shouldn't feel. It is okay to be depressed after an abortion, okay to be deeply affected by it."

"You know," he says, a bit wistfully. "We have gotten so 'liberated,' it's getting hard to acknowledge any bad feelings about sex. A lot of people really need permission to feel guilty."

Of Death

When Maria took an overdose of sleeping pills and died, it was a shock to everyone who knew her.

"Sure, she was moody now and then," her sister, Betsy, said. "But I'd always managed to kid her out of it . . . or scold her a little bit and tell her to quit feeling sorry for herself and acting like a drag."

"*I* never took it that seriously," her boyfriend, Will, admitted sadly. "I mean once, for the hell of it, I made a big play for one of her friends—right in front of her. It didn't mean anything, but Maria went into the bathroom and took a half a dozen aspirins. That was about a year and a half ago. Nothing else like that happened until a couple of months ago when she began pushing me about getting engaged and I said I'm not ready and she locked herself in the bathroom, took a razor, and made a couple of little scratches on her wrists. I guess I did get a little scared; afterwards, I said, 'okay, let's say we're engaged to be engaged for the time being, okay?' and she said okay and that was the end of it, I thought.

"And it was only last Friday that she asked if I was seeing someone else. I said, yeah. I figured why lie. Well, Maria didn't even act upset. She told me to go home, that she had to study for an exam, and then she killed herself—just like that."

Young suicides like Maria's are no longer the statistical rarity that they were even a couple of decades ago. In fact, the phenomenon has reached what the experts call an epidemic—and the number continues to rise. There are various theories about *why* it's happening so much more these days: about how society has changed and how much harder it is to feel connected and worthwhile.

But whatever the cause, the big problem is knowing what to do: how to recognize and reach a person who is suffering so much that he thinks suicide is the only way out.

There is widespread concern about this problem, and plenty of action to go with it, as more and more churches, hospitals, community groups, and other organizations are starting suicide-prevention clinics and hotlines. One of the most impressive groups is a nonreligious one called The Samaritans, which began in England in the 1950s and now operates a number of centers elsewhere, including one in Boston.

The Samaritans believe that "everyone should have the dignity of control over their own life—or death." They recognize that a suicide attempt or gesture is almost always a cry for help, and that the caller who says, "I am going to kill myself" usually means, "I'm afraid I may kill myself—please help me."

"The Samaritans do not claim to save lives," says the Boston center's director, Monica Dickens. "They try to help the caller in saving his own life, and to support him in finding a renewal of spirit that may eventually make his life more worth living."

When someone drops in at the center or phones their twenty-four-hour hotline, the Samaritans' carefully selected and specially trained volunteers steer clear of any canned response, any Pollyanna pep talk. Nor do they practice therapy (though professional therapists praise their work and refer certain patients to them). What they do is "befriend" the caller; offering concern, attention, and moral support in a session which may last a few minutes or several hours. There may be one session or several, all according to the needs of the individual caller.

This kind of intervention seems to help in a variety of ways:

• *Opening the lines of communication.* The fact that a caller doesn't even have to give his name or show his face makes it possible for some very shy or frightened people to make that essential contact with a person who cares. The same holds true for someone who isn't usually all that withdrawn, but who feels very embarrassed and uptight about having to ask for help. All of a sudden, he, too, has someone he can talk to, someone who understands, who listens, who doesn't think the caller is a reject or a failure, *and* someone who doesn't get impatient if a caller is a little bit defensive or confused or disorganized as he tries to explain what's bothering him.

"I guess I'm not so isolated after all" is the very relieved feeling that many callers get. They know that they can call again if they should need to.

• *Easing the panic of the moment.* Talking out a seemingly insoluble problem with a volunteer can often take the terrifying edge off it, make it seem more manageable, less hopeless. This can be very important to someone who is feeling troubled but is not in the habit of talking about private things.

• *Talking about the suicidal feeling itself*—contrary

to what most people believe—can be extremely therapeutic. The average person who has not given
conscious thought to his own feelings about death
and self-destruction (as the Samaritans, in their
training, *have* done) may get angry or embarrassed
and tend to shut the person up, rather than encourage him to talk. There is an erroneous belief that
letting a person talk about committing suicide will
encourage him to carry out the act. People involved
in the study and treatment of suicidal behavior say
that asking a person in a frank and kindly way if he
has thought about ending his life isn't at all like
saying, "Jump, jump!" to a person on a window
ledge. On the contrary, it gives the person permission to air what he has been keeping inside: getting
these forbidden feelings out can be a vast relief.

• *Assessing the urgency.* There is no foolproof way
for a psychiatrist, psychologist, or any hotline staffer
to know exactly how close to the brink a caller is.
A halfhearted suicide attempt may look harmless,
but even a mere gesture which *in itself* wouldn't kill
a fly might be a crucial warning of what a person
plans to do.

"A suicidal crisis," says New York psychiatrist Dr.
Leonard Moss, "is a self-limiting disease. It's like
a cold in the sense that you get it, it reaches a peak,
and then it goes away." But just because a person
tends to feel much better once the crisis has passed
doesn't mean that he is out of the woods. "Suicidal

feelings are a sign of unresolved problems," says Dr. Moss. "That crisis tends to recur—and get worse —unless there is some substantial change in the person's life situation."

People who staff the special suicide prevention services—and many therapists and counselors elsewhere—are trained to recognize certain clues as particular danger signals.

First, a history of suicide in the family can sometimes make the prospect of doing it or trying it more real to some people. Also, a long personal history of loneliness, of being unable, even in early childhood, to relate to others is a common theme among suicidal adolescents and young adults.

Another common trait among the suicidal seems to be a deep sense of failure in never having managed to live up to the rigid standards and too-high expectations their parents set for them. As Dr. Michael L. Peck and Dr. Albert Schrut of the Los Angeles Suicide Prevention Center put it, "These parental expectations of students who commit suicide are far more than the usual wishes for success that most parents have for their children. They represent a total lack of acceptance of their children as they are.

"Children who commit suicide find that their efforts to express their feelings of unhappiness, frustration, or failure are totally unacceptable to their parents. Their feelings are ignored, denied, or met by defensive hostility. 'What have you got to be unhappy about; you have everything; we don't beat you; what do you want?' Such a response seems to occur often in these families, driving the children into further isolation with the feeling that 'something' is terribly wrong with them."

Those are some of the underlying themes that someone doing suicide prevention counseling might be particularly alert to, *especially* if any such information comes across *along with* an imminent danger sign such as:

(1) the impending anniversary of some major loss, like the death—or desertion—of a parent

(2) a recent untreated suicide attempt

(3) the recent death or loss of someone important, or the breakup of a very big and important relationship

(4) a specific, immediate, and *concrete* plan for the suicide: (not "Some day I'm really going to kill myself," but "I'm going to go down to the basement after supper and hang myself from a pipe with some rope I've been saving.")

How far can this intervention go?

The suicide-prevention workers' intelligent and compassionate responses can help enormously, but they do have certain limitations. The workers can listen and they can sympathize, soothe, and indeed befriend a person. They can actively intervene. But they cannot keep someone alive against his will.

As for helping to keep a person safe from future suicidal crises, even the nonprofessional trained worker can do a great deal, Dr. Moss says. "Just how much may depend on the extent of a caller's own ability to focus on and look at his suicidal effort, his own capacity to heal, gain insight and use it in changing his behavior."

More than simply a rescue squad

The crisis-center worker will sometimes suggest professional help—i.e., therapy—for the caller. This can be an excellent opportunity to reverse a trend towards self-destruction; a chance to get to the heart of the matter. Dr. Moss says, "Sometimes in therapy the suicidal problem goes away as you begin to focus on other themes: the problems *underneath* the despair that made a person feel so very desperate."

At any rate, it's worth noting that of all the people who seek help for suicidal feelings, the vast majority seem to be able to get the help they need—help to find less drastic ways of coping with their problems and themselves, help to feel like an independent—but connected—member of the human race.

8

Squaring it

Just because you've opened your mind to trying therapy doesn't mean that the people around you are going to be 100 percent supportive—or even willing to tolerate your decision. Some of the nicest people are still in the stone age when it comes to accepting emotions as *real things.* You are going to have to work out some idea of what and how much you're going to say to which people, and when you're going to keep your mouth shut altogether.

Caution: Parents

No question about it: parents are sticky, and you have to use incredible tact in dealing with them. Sometimes you haven't any choice, but when you do, it is most helpful to have them on your side. You need them there not just for emotional comfort, but so that you don't have the hassle of sneaking out to your appointments or charging off in a spirit of defiance. Many therapists require parental approval, both in the sense of financial backing and because some agencies and individuals are personally unwilling to treat—if not legally barred from treating—minors without a parent's say-so. And, of course, if you're interested in family therapy, you've got to persuade the folks to jump right in with you.

We're not saying that you're totally at your parents' mercy in whether or not you're to get help, but it broadens your options and makes more kinds of help available to you if you *can* get your parents to see the value of it.

Why should any scheming be necessary? Ideally, parents should be glad to see their kids reaching for a kind of balance and maturity. Well, sure, *if* they really see it in those terms. Many parents won't or can't, no matter how diplomatically you lay it out. They mean well, they love you, but therapy is just too alien—or too threatening—an idea. Still, it's up to you and very *much* in your interest to *try* to get them to understand and accept your wish to go to work on yourself.

Here are some of the parental hang-ups that you may have to work around:

(1) Guilt

Most parents are ready to blame themselves for anything that smacks of an imperfection in their offspring's development. In other words, your interest in seeing a therapist might seem to them like an accusation of some failure on their part. It is a great mistake to think that you can capitalize on that. Whether or not they are responsible for your present hang-ups, it is not only kind but pragmatic to do a little bending-over-backwards reassuring.

It's not even enough to tell them that you know they didn't *mean* anything; guilt tends to make people belligerent. To deny their fears, your parents might say your distress is all in your imagination or it's a lot of nonsense. What you've got to do is *help* them dismiss the thought that you are a basket case or that they are at fault in any way. If they ask you what is wrong and you feel that you have to go into the specifics, you can put it in terms of how rapidly the world is evolving, how you need to prepare yourself for coping with all the rapid change, the turmoil, all the weird stuff going on out there. . . .

(2) The empty nest

Some parents argue against therapy for their off-spring because they say it's too expensive or not necessary. But their *real* objection is that they're scared. In this case, scared that the child, once liberated, will outgrow his parents, reject them, and find that he has no use for them anymore. It's a fairly common fear in parents who tend to hold onto their kids a little too tightly. Rather than confronting them, it's a better idea for you to be super-tactful and let them know subtly that one of your goals in therapy is arriving at a better, richer, and less antagonistic relationship with them.

(3) "But you're so healthy"

Your parents might sincerely feel that you seem much too sunny and wholesome to need anything as "dire" as professional help. What you'd need to do here is explain that it's entirely possible to feel bad without showing it, and professional help is not a dire remedy at all but a preventive measure.

(4) "Get off your butt"

If your parents are of the brisk-walks-and-quit-feeling-sorry-for-yourself school of "therapy," it's a help to try and get the idea across to them that you are emphatically *not* looking to be coddled out of your dilemma. What you want, you might tell them, is an opportunity to get yourself straightened out, back on the track. You're willing to work at it. You might even hint that you're willing to go through the sometimes painful ordeal of therapy in order to become the nicer, better, more responsible human being that they've been wishing you'd shape up into. (Note: Be careful not to overdo this. If they think you're being sarcastic, it'll just start a fight.)

(5) Explain why it has to be private

Many parents are so convinced of what you're doing and so eager to help that they want to jump right in and participate. The only thing they can't understand is why you aren't giving them detailed reports on every single phase of your fantastic metamorphosis. It is up to you to explain the need for privacy: how it's an important part of producing an atmosphere of comfort which is so necessary to the good work you're doing with your shrink. Once they realize that no revolution is being plotted during your top-secret sessions (and that no one thinks that they are neglecting you by staying out of it), they will probably calm down.

What if your friends find out?

It's natural, especially at first, to feel like you've got to tell everyone in sight. After all, it's not shameful, right?

You might crack jokes about it and be flippant—"Hurry up my Big Mac, Charlie. I can't keep the headshrinker waiting." Or you might be terribly earnest and intense, wanting to explain it *all*, to anyone who happens to sit next to you in the cafeteria.

Actually, it's not unwise to keep the fact of your therapy quiet, even though there isn't any shame attached. Even if your friends would be entirely sympathetic, they might get a little too mother-hennish, asking questions all the time and expecting progress reports.

Ironically, it's people who've had initial qualms about therapy who can become the major nuisances about it. Take Rachel, for example. She was so enthusiastic about how much better she felt since she began therapy that she went around button-holing everyone and telling them—with missionary zeal—how they absolutely couldn't afford *not* to go and get their heads shrunk because it's such a marvelous experience, and so on and so forth.

Robin, another unrestrained enthusiast, took *her* pro-shrink crusade a step further. She actually conducted her own unsolicited minisessions on her friends. ("Oh, Peter, I'm afraid you have a very unhealthy ego and your fear of women is obvious under all that bluster . . .")

Even when you are very discreet and selective in telling people, you may have to cope with an occasional reaction that feels like a stinging slap in the face. Take Sarah. When she told her young and supposedly with-it assistant principal that she would be going to a psychologist on Tuesday afternoons and would need permission to leave study hall twenty minutes early, he looked at her with a leer and said, "Gee, Sarah, I knew you were crazy, but I didn't know you were *that* crazy."

So—it is not always the *obvious* fuddy-duddies who'll give you a rough time. All you can do is take it in stride, and maybe feel a little sorry for people who are so petrified, so narrow-minded, and so out of touch.

Of course, if you're asked *why* you go, you don't have to describe your particular malaise. You can simply say that you're getting rid of a hang-up or working out a problem or seeking insight. Or even just getting liberated.

As for the oversolicitous and needlers alike, you can keep them all politely at bay. It's your business and yours alone, something intimate and private. You don't owe anyone an explanation.

What if you really feel that a friend could use the help?

"This is often quite hard," says Mickey Maley, past coordinator of the excellent Walk-in Counseling Center in Minneapolis. "It can be a terrible strain knowing someone needs help but won't get it. Still, it's up to that person to decide if and when he needs help. It usually doesn't work to force someone to get help for any kind of problem. If that person is making too much of a demand on you with his problem, the best thing to do is to tell that person that you don't feel qualified to help him, or that it is beginning to worry you too much, or it is too much of a demand, and that you think he should get help. Tell him you know a good place for him to go and offer to give him a ride. That's really all you can do. You realize that's not much of an answer but it's the sad truth. You can't force people to seek help. But you can encourage them, and your honesty with this person is the best favor you can give."

9

How to square it with yourself: checking out the results

How can you tell when you're finished?

Other than arbitrarily setting a time limit before you begin (which some people do), you can usually rely on your own gut feelings. It's best, of course, if you can take those feelings with a grain or two of salt.

- *Feeling better*

Is that enough? It depends on what you came for. Once in a while, the shrinker and client are both so eager to make it happen that they see good results before any changes have really taken place. But let's assume that the relief is real. If you went to the therapist in order to get relief from a particular problem, such as a dangerous habit or a fear that immobilizes you, then feeling good is certainly enough. But if you went with a wish to dig deeper, to do more heavy-duty analyzing and reorganizing, you may want to hold out for greater results.

- *Feeling no better*

If you've been going for therapy for a while and you're really working at it, yet you still feel that nothing is happening, it might be a problem with the therapist. You certainly might mention it to him.

We're not suggesting that you keep pulling up the radishes to check on how they're growing. Just that you might take a look now and then at what has or hasn't changed in your life, in your head, in your dealings with other people. It might be time to switch therapists, try something different like group instead of individual therapy (or vice versa), or it may be time to stop.

Are you being patient enough? A lot of people clearly understand that therapy cannot remove all "warts" or impart any extraordinary powers. These people are realistic enough in terms of what they expect to accomplish, but they think that what's going to happen is going to happen right away in a mere session or two. As a result, they feel rushed and nervous about "stating the case"—and extremely impatient if the therapist doesn't share their sense of urgency and produce miraculously quick changes. You can "feel better fast," but for "more lasting relief" it will take more time.

The point is, maybe it works out in some television dramas, but in real life you don't get everything important out in a giant verbal upchuck or two. Nor do you suddenly say "Aha!" and shed your fears or malaise so neatly. Therapy is a process of probing, discovering, relearning; none of that can happen instantly. It's a matter of growth which—just like in gardening—can't be coerced.

On the other hand, if by "no better" you mean that you have not ascended to a state of bliss, then you were misled about what to expect—which is not so unusual! Even the most sophisticated people with all kinds of knowledge of psychology still, when it comes to their own personal situation, harbor some rather grandiose secret hopes. Here are a couple of examples:

1. *Superperson.* The fantasy that you'll be competent and on top of things after you've weeded out the hang-ups and imperfections. You'll feel you'll never again be lazy, humiliated, irrational, lonely, upset, or anything but a terrifically serene and self-contained adult, enjoying a glorious existence.

2. *Superbrain.* This one is a little less prevalent, but there are still plenty around like Jed, the perennial class brain who "had to" get all A's and used to study even on the school bus and at birthday parties when he was in grade school. Jed, who could have used the opportunity therapy offered in order to learn about whether his fierce academic drive was what he really *wanted* to concentrate all his energy on, lost interest and quit after just one appointment. Why? Because he found out that therapy would not serve as a mental vacuum cleaner, sweeping up all

distractions and impediments to his intellectual concentration and achievement.

Therapy can't insulate you against feeling rotten. It can help you avoid excessive rotten-feelings-inducing situations—and help you find better ways of coping when those situations are inevitable.

• *Feeling worse*

This may be a good sign that things are getting stirred up. Digging does hurt, but that doesn't mean it isn't worth some discomfort to get to where you want to be. (If you have a splinter in your foot, it'll surely hurt more to get it out than to let it stay in, but you'll feel a lot more comfortable in the long run.)

Maybe, like Anna, your "new muscles" are what's giving you the pain. Anna had always been exceedingly meek, letting everyone take advantage of her. In therapy, for the first time, she was really starting to stand up for herself. While it was an improvement for her to be acting more assertive, it took her a while before the new non-doormat role began to feel comfortable.

• *Feeling like quitting*

It may be exactly the right thing to do, but rather than impulsively skipping out on what you've already put so much into, it's a great idea to hold off your decision until you've had a chance to talk it over with your therapist—especially if you've been going for a while. He might very well agree!

The tricky thing is that it's very natural to *feel* like everything has come out in the wash and/or fallen into place, right before a big flood of intense new feelings emerge. Of course, you can't know that in advance. All you know is that you suddenly feel *very much* like quitting. But even if it turns out that you quit a bit prematurely, it isn't any irrevocable act. If you find, in retrospect, that you haven't gotten all you wanted to get from therapy, and you feel that you might like to go back (even once or twice), that is perfectly okay and a lot of people do just that.

Coping with what everybody else thinks

If you were to take a consensus of your friends and family, you'd probably find that they couldn't agree on whether your new hairstyle is an improvement or not—much less be objective about the changes inside your head!

Again, the problem is one of perspective:

• *Jamie, the life-of-the-party,* may, after some therapy, seem like a bit of a drag. After all, now he can tolerate his own company and doesn't feel that he has to work so hard at entertaining everyone. Some of his "friends" who depended on his party mood to jolly *them* up would swear that therapy had "really messed up old Jamie."

- *Len, the dutiful son,* won't win any mental health medals from his mother! He is starting to think for himself and to make decisions according to his own judgment, not just acting out of blind obedience or equally blind defiance.

"You used to be so sweet," his mother might complain if Len says that he has things to do and can't stay home with her and watch television on a Saturday night. Len might have twinges of guilt when his mother puts on her wounded-widow look, but it would be a shame if he were to take her very biased opinion of his therapy to heart.

- *Kitty, who had been going steady* with Grant since seventh grade, finds that now, at eighteen and with the help of counseling, she has become more confident, more curious, more interested in tasting life. In short, she would like to date others, at least for a while. Grant, who had approved of Kitty's decision to try therapy (because he had mistakenly hoped that she would become "less argumentative, more settled") is disappointed and thinks that Kitty's therapist has "made her more screwed up."

The $64,000 question: does *therapy work?*

What you want to know, of course, isn't "Does therapy always work for everyone?" but "Will it work for me?" It is of little value to you to know whether Joe had great results or lousy ones. Even if Joe had the grandest and most persuasive testimonial to offer, it wouldn't mean anything to anyone but Joe. First of all, we wouldn't know how well he would have done *anyway* without therapy, just growing on his own. And then, even if we were convinced that Joe had gotten dynamite results, Joe is only one individual and his case wouldn't tell us a thing about how well someone else would do— even with the very same therapist.

Still, most studies have shown that therapy can and often does make a positive and measurable difference. In one experiment, forty students who had applied for counseling at their university were divided into two groups: half were given individual therapy right away, while the others were asked to wait three months. At the end of that period, the twenty who had been treated showed much more improvement in the way they were feeling and coping than the twenty who had not been treated. Such documented studies can be found in many professional journals. You can pile up all kinds of evidence, proof, and testimonials, but there isn't any guarantee that therapy will work for you. To a small extent, as the New York Mets would say, "You gotta believe!"

Sometimes it doesn't work

Therapy is no panacea; it will not work for everyone, and it certainly will not work for everyone all the time. You might decide that it's not for you or not for you right now. This is a perfectly valid decision.

However, when therapy *does* seem like the right thing, there are benefits that derive from the therapeutic process itself. For instance:

(1) Emotional awareness and insight. Once you get into therapy, you learn to be a great deal more observant and discriminating—both about your own actions and about the treatment you've been putting up with from others.

(2) An awareness of how accessible therapy is. You've learned how available and unarduous it is. You know where to find it and what's involved. You know you can take advantage of it if you should need to in the future *before* you feel like you are on the verge of cracking up.

(3) A reusable process. Therapy is a skill, a technique, a way of facing up to your feelings and problems without folding up, running away, or harming yourself.

Some fringe benefits
You might not be reckless, but a little more spontaneous and daring in your behavior now that you've begun to see that you don't have to be liked and approved of by everyone you know. You may be more tolerant of yourself—and others. Now, instead of expecting perfection and ending up furious and

disappointed each time the human flaws appear, you can accept the Real World. You can risk your self-image by speaking up in class or at the dinner table without worrying about whether "they" think you're brilliant or dumb. (You're *you!*)

It may even surprise you to find that certain attitudes you held or a particular life-style you adhered to are not really you at all. Maybe you don't really want to be a lawyer, but would love to be a railroad engineer or a cab driver. As you get better acquainted with yourself, you learn to follow your inclinations, instead of taking some merely logical or probable course set out for you by your parents.

10
Finding a good one

How can you tell if a therapist is any good?

There is no absolute or magical criterion or quality control for therapists. But there are enough guidelines you can go by—official and unofficial—so that you don't have to waste time with some sincere-sounding incompetent.

• *Sizing him up/Checking him out*

There are some objective standards you can check, such as the person's credentials: what training has he had? how long? how intensive? what kind? where? who trained him? how much experience has he had since his training? what kind of clients does he have? He doesn't, of course, have to be a specialist in your kind of problem, but it is reassuring to know that he hasn't been dealing exclusively with middle-aged businessmen or children in hospitals, for example.

While you would rightly stay away from any so-called therapist who advertises or verbally promises some miracle results, it's also a good idea to avoid respectable-sounding quacks. They abound! In most states, anyone can call himself a "counselor." Therefore, unless your prospective therapist has been recommended by someone you trust, is affiliated with a reputable clinic, or belongs to a real professional organization, you might want to be a little wary.

You may certainly question a prospective therapist on his background and special qualifications for helping you. *That is your right even if the treatment is free of charge!* You can also ask what, if any, professional organization he belongs to. If he's a bona fide member of one of the major professional groups, he won't be offended by your asking.

But that is not the whole story! We don't mean to say that diplomas and a seal of approval from the person's colleagues are anywhere near enough. Dr. So-and-so might be famous, but if he strikes you as an oaf or seems patronizing, forget it! There are other therapists. The main thing to remember is that *you* are the one who's doing the hiring.

Here are some types you'll probably want to avoid. Fortunately, they are in the minority. Still, forewarned is forearmed.

• *The therapist with all the answers*

If the therapist immediately wants to give you a prescription for what you should do to remedy your life, if he's bossy and seems to see his role as a combination "how-to" manual and friendly neighborhood fountain of wisdom, you may want to look elsewhere. "Advice," says one therapist we know, "is worth exactly nothing."

• *The therapist with an axe to grind*

If he seems to be pushing a certain kind of lifestyle or a political viewpoint or attitude, it's probably a good idea to trade him in. He can get you all muddled up, confusing matters of opinion or taste with maturity and mental health. He may be intolerant of any growth on your part that is not in line with his thinking. All in all, he is much more apt to be pushy and didactic than helpful. (It's not that he shouldn't have opinions, just that he shouldn't wear them on his sleeve to the extent that he gives yours the brush-off.) The point of therapy is to examine your own feelings and beliefs, not acquire someone else's.

• *The professional good guy*

Naturally you want a therapist who is concerned enough to care about what you are hoping to accomplish, wants you to succeed, and believes that you can.

But if he talks a great deal about how much he wants to help you, he might be too busy trying to save the world to take the time to help you sort out what you need to learn about yourself. Also, if he seems to want to "help" you in the sense of improving you, he is essentially a reformer—which nobody needs.

Your own gut feelings: just how trustworthy are they?

As we've been saying, it's not just *what* a therapist is, but *who* he is that counts. Just as it's not enough to be on the faculty of a famous university if the guy is stuffy and remote, it's also not enough for him to wear love beads and have long, bushy hair if he's too busy being "with-it" to really listen to *you*. It doesn't matter how impressive or right his credentials are, how good his track record has been, or even how many of your friends have told you he's the greatest; *unless you feel comfortable* none of this matters. You must feel that the therapist is "all there," attentive, and entirely alert to what you are trying to get out.

What if your dislike of a particular therapist is based on something irrelevant or silly?

The therapist reminds you unpleasantly of your Uncle Waldo? Maybe it isn't a mere physical resemblance or similar mannerism that bothers you, but the fact that you've correctly intuited in the therapist the same kind of condescending manner, hostile sense of humor, or pickiness that annoys you in Waldo.

On the other hand, if the therapist in question is just the latest in a series of rejects, you might want to talk it out instead of just leaving. It might make you feel better to make sure that you aren't inadvertently projecting imaginary Waldo-like characteristics on therapists in general. In which case, it *might* be a good idea to express it to a therapist, as this too can be grist for the mill.

Sources

On your own. If you want to keep your search entirely under wraps, you can always try a local hotline and/or drop-in counseling center in your area. That way, if you want, you can start out incognito.

If there isn't any such service locally, you might try the National Runaway Switchboard (800–621–4000, free of charge). Even if things aren't desperate enough to drive you out of the house, you can still call them for help. They have a great and voluminous list of local referrals for counseling help in problems ranging from abusive parents to drugs, problem pregnancy, suicidal feelings, legal hassles, and medical dilemmas. They also will recommend a runaway house or other safe temporary lodging.

Ask someone you trust. Anyone and everyone, in fact. Check with friends, your minister, a peer counselor, guidance counselor, doctor, or anyone else

who might know. The advantage of a personal referral is that they can usually refer you to a *person*
at some agency rather than just the agency.

Shop around. No matter who is acting as your
consultant, it's especially helpful if he can suggest
more than one possibility so that you have a choice
and an immediate basis for comparison.

If you're having trouble finding good leads or
would just like some extra ones, you can write and
ask the following organizations for any local referrals.

(1) American Association of Marriage and
    Family Counselors
    225 Yale Avenue
    Claremont, California 91711
(2) American Association of Pastoral Coun-
    selors
    3 West 29 Street
    New York, New York 10001
(3) Family Service Association of America
    44 East 23 Street
    New York, New York 10010

For the official word on fees, state laws regarding
minors, professional ethics, or any other aspect of
getting therapy or counseling where you are, you
can write to the appropriate mental health authority
in any state, and in Puerto Rico, the Virgin Islands,
American Samoa, or the Trust Territories of the
Pacific Islands.

ALABAMA

Commissioner for Community Programs
State Department of Mental Health
502 Washington Avenue
Montgomery, Alabama 36104
205-269-7494

ALASKA

Director, Division of Mental Health
State Department of Health and Welfare
Alaska Office Building
Pouch H, Health and Welfare Building
Juneau, Alaska 99801
907-277-6551

ARIZONA

Commissioner for Mental Health Services
State Department of Health
State Office Building
1624 West Adams Street
Phoenix, Arizona 85007
602-271-5572

ARKANSAS

Director
Arkansas State Hospital
4313 West Markham Street
Little Rock, Arkansas 72201
501-666-0181

CALIFORNIA

Director
State Department of Mental Hygiene
744 P Street
Sacramento, California 95814
916-445-1605

COLORADO

Director, Division of Mental Health
Department of Institutions
328 State Services Building
Denver, Colorado 80203
303-892-2595

CONNECTICUT

Commissioner
State Department of Mental Health
90 Washington Street
Hartford, Connecticut 06115
203-566-3650
203-566-3651

DELAWARE

Director, Division of Mental Health
Department of Health & Social Service
300 Newport Gap Pike
Wilmington, Delaware 19808
302-988-0453

DISTRICT OF COLUMBIA

Director
Mental Health Administration
Department of Human Resources
1875 Connecticut Avenue, N.W.
Room 822
Washington, D.C. 20009
202-629-3438

FLORIDA

Director
Community Mental Health Services
Division of Mental Health
Department of Health & Rehabilitative Service
Larson Building
200 East Gaines Street
Tallahassee, Florida 32304
904-222-8007

GEORGIA

Director, Division of Mental Health
Department of Public Health
State Office Building
47 Trinity Avenue, S.W.
Atlanta, Georgia 30334
404-656-4908

HAWAII

Director, Division of Mental Health
State Department of Health
P.O. Box 3378
Honolulu, Hawaii 96801
808-548-2811

IDAHO

Director
Mental Health Division
Idaho Department of Health
State House
Boise, Idaho 83701
208-964-3410

ILLINOIS

Director
State Department of Mental Health
160 North LaSalle Street, Rm. 1500
Chicago, Illinois 60601
312-525-4977

INDIANA

Commissioner
State Department of Mental Health
1315 West 10th Street
Indianapolis, Indiana 46207
317-633-5490

IOWA

Director
Department of Social Services
Bureau of Mental Health Services
Lucas State Office Building
Des Moines, Iowa 50319
319-353-3901

KANSAS

Director of Institutions
State Department of Social Welfare
State Office Building
Topeka, Kansas 66612
913-296-3774

KENTUCKY

Commissioner
State Department of Mental Health
P.O. Box 678
Frankfort, Kentucky 40601
502-564-3810

LOUISIANA

Commissioner of Mental Health
State Department of Hospitals
State Capitol Building
655 North Fifth Street
Baton Rouge, Louisiana 70804
504-389-5366

MAINE

Director
State Department of Mental Health & Corrections
411 State Office Building
Augusta, Maine 04330
207-289-3161

MARYLAND

Commissioner of Mental Hygiene
Maryland Department of Health & Mental Hygiene
State Office Building
301 West Preston Street
Baltimore, Maryland 21201
301-383-3010 Ext. 562

MASSACHUSETTS

Commissioner
State Department of Mental Health
190 Portland Street
Boston, Massachusetts 02114
617-727-5600

MICHIGAN

Director
State Department of Mental Health
Lewis Cass Building
Lansing, Michigan 48913
517-373-1320

MINNESOTA

Director, Medical Services Division
State Department of Public Welfare
Centennial Office Building
St. Paul, Minnesota 55101
612-296-2697

MISSISSIPPI

Director, Mental Health Services
State Board of Health
Felix Underwood Building
Jackson, Mississippi 39205
601-354-6628

MISSOURI

Director
Division of Mental Health
722 Jefferson Street
Jefferson City, Missouri 65101
314-635-0251

MONTANA

Superintendent & Director
State Division of Mental Hygiene
Montana State Hospital
Warm Springs, Montana 59756
406-693-2221

NEBRASKA

Director of Health
State Department of Health
State Office Building
Lincoln, Nebraska 68509
402-471-2231

NEVADA

Administrator, Division of Mental Health
State Department of Health, Welfare & Rehabili-
tation
Nevada State Hospital
P.O. Box 2460
Reno, Nevada 89505
702-882-7593

NEW HAMPSHIRE

Director, Division of Mental Health
State Department of Health & Welfare
105 Pleasant Street
Concord, New Hampshire 03301
603-271-2366

NEW JERSEY

Chief
Bureau of Special Community Mental Health
  Services
Division of Mental Health & Hospitals
State Department of Institutions & Agencies
State Office Building
P.O. Box 1237
Trenton, New Jersey 08625
609-292-3717

NEW MEXICO

Director, Mental Health & Authority
Department of Hospitals & Institutions
Lamy Building
425 Old Santa Fe Trail
Santa Fe, New Mexico 87501
505-827-2595

NEW YORK

Commissioner, Division of Local Services
New York State Department of Mental Hygiene
44 Holland Avenue
Albany, New York 12208
518-474-4403

NORTH CAROLINA

Secretary
Department of Human Resources
P.O. Box 26327
325 N. Salisbury Street
Raleigh, North Carolina 27611
919-829-7011

NORTH DAKOTA

State Health Officer
State Department of Health
State Capitol
Bismarck, North Dakota 58501
701-224-2372

OHIO

Commissioner
State Department of Mental Hygiene & Correction
State Office Building
Columbus, Ohio 43215
614-469-3543

OKLAHOMA

Director
State Department of Mental Health
P.O. Box 53277, Capitol Station
Oklahoma City, Oklahoma 73105
405-521-2151

OREGON

Director
Department of Human Resources
2570 Center Street N.E.
Salem, Oregon 97310
503-378-2460

PENNSYLVANIA

Deputy, Secretary for Mental Health & Mental
   Retardation
State Department of Public Welfare
Room 310
Health & Welfare Building
Harrisburg, Pennsylvania 17120
717-787-6443

RHODE ISLAND

Director
Department of Mental Health & Mental Retarda-
   tion & Hospitals
The Aime J. Forand Building
New London Avenue
Cranston, Rhode Island 02834
401-463-7400

SOUTH CAROLINA

Commissioner
State Department of Mental Health
P.O. Box 485
Columbia, South Carolina 29202
803-256-9911

SOUTH DAKOTA

Director
State Commission of Mental Health & Mental
    Retardation
Suite 6, Equitable Building
116 N. Euclid
Pierre, South Dakota 57501
605-224-3438

TENNESSEE

Director of Community Services
State Department of Mental Health
300 Cordell Hull Building
Nashville, Tennessee 37219
615-741-3107

TEXAS

Commissioner for Mental Health
Texas Department of Mental Health and Mental
    Retardation
Capitol Station
P.O. Box 12668
Austin, Texas 78711
512-454-3761

UTAH

Director, Division of Mental Health
State Department of Social Services
520 East Fourth, South
Salt Lake City, Utah 84102
801-328-5331

VERMONT

Commissioner
State Department of Mental Health
State Office Building
Montpelier, Vermont 05602
802-828-2481

VIRGINIA

Commissioner
State Department of Mental Hygiene & Hospitals
P.O. Box 1797
Richmond, Virginia 23214
703-770-3921

WASHINGTON

Chief, Office of Mental Health
State Mental Health Authority
Division of Social Services
Department of Social & Health Services
P.O. Box 1788
Olympia, Washington 98501
206-753-5406

WEST VIRGINIA

Director
State Department of Mental Health
State Capitol Building
Charleston, West Virginia 25305
304-345-3414

WISCONSIN

Administrator, Division of Mental Hygiene
State Department of Health & Social Services
State Office Building
1 West Wilson Street
Madison, Wisconsin 53702
608-266-1538

WYOMING

Director, Mental Health & Mental Retardation
 Services
State Department of Health & Social Services
State Office Building
Cheyenne, Wyoming 82001
307-777-7275

GUAM

Director, Division of Mental Health
Mental Health Services
Guam Memorial Hospital
Government of Guam, P.O. Box AX
Agana, Guam 96910

PUERTO RICO

Secretary for Mental Health & Mental Retardation
Commonwealth of Puerto Rico
Department of Health
Ponce de Leon Avenue
San Juan, Puerto Rico 00908
809-767-9222

AMERICAN SAMOA

Director
Department of Medical Services
Government of American Samoa
Pago-Pago, Tutuila, American Samoa 96920

TRUST TERRITORY OF THE PACIFIC ISLANDS

Chief, Mental Health Division
Office of the High Commissioner
Trust Territory of the Pacific Islands
Saipan, Mariana Islands 96950

VIRGIN ISLANDS

Director, Division of Mental Health
Department of Health
P.O. Box 1442
St. Thomas, Virgin Islands 00801
809-774-4888

If you would like to help other young people find
better access to counseling help, you might be able

to get involved in and/or help start a peer counseling program in your area. For more on this, you might want to contact any or all of the following sources:

(1) National Youth Alternatives Project
1830 Connecticut Avenue N.W.
Washington, D.C. 20009

Based on the idea that all youth have the right to human service programs which are accessible and acceptable to them, National Youth Alternatives Project offers these services:

a. helps groups attempting to establish, expand, or evaluate innovative services aimed at meeting the needs of young people who have rejected or who have been rejected by traditional social institutions.
b. offers training and technical assistance to staff members of runaway centers, crisis intervention centers, hotlines, free clinics, drug and alcohol counseling centers, and so on.
c. provides voluminous information on youth programs through the Youth Alternatives Clearinghouse which also maintains a resource library of youth information and which has published several related manuals and information packets.

d. publishes *Youth Alternatives,* a monthly ($10 per year) newsletter on policymaking and funding activities that directly affect youth and youth services.

(2) National Commission on Resources for Youth, Inc.
36 West 44 Street
New York, N. Y. 10036

Here they have an information clearinghouse on youth participation programs (including peer counseling) in communities and schools. They have videotapes, films, and lots of write-ups of existing programs. You can write for their free quarterly newsletter, *Resources for Youth.* They can give you ideas for workable projects and refer you to people who can help you get them off the ground.

(3) The Youth and Student Affairs Program
Planned Parenthood Federation of America, Inc.
810 Seventh Avenue
New York, N. Y. 10019

They offer a free bi-monthly newsletter called *Getting It Together* on innovative programs, legal aspects, seminars, conferences, and new materials regarding sexual health and counseling services for young people. Also, if you write them about your project (or one you would like to help get started), they'll send you information on what's involved in starting a birth control center or organizing a student sex information project within a high school.

11
Putting it all together

If you've read this far, you already know a lot more about therapy and counseling than most people do. You know, for example, that it doesn't take craziness or near-disaster to warrant a little professional help: you don't even have to have a specific reason for going—and you don't owe anyone an "explanation." Just wanting to clarify something, or share what's inside you, or get in touch with your feelings can be enough.

Also, you are free of the myths that say a shrink will take away your own uniqueness or make you into something that you're not. And you know that therapy doesn't have to mean a great time or money commitment. (You can do a lot in just a few sessions, and the fee—if there is one—is often a pay-what-you-can afford one.)

Maybe you're not inclined to make a beeline to

the shrinker. There are sources of help around you—
right in your own "natural" environment. There are
clergy people, the family doctor, school guidance
counselors. There are also telephone hot lines, both
local and national, and your own peers available
for counseling at school or somewhere in the community. Any of them might be able to give you the
kind of help you're seeking, but if not, they can usually be counted on for a referral to someone who can
fill the bill.

What about the professional shrink? The profession has become much more diverse and flexible in
the past several years. Nowadays, your "best" therapist may or may not be a psychiatrist—or a psychologist, for that matter. The field has broadened to
include pastoral counselors, social workers, and
other *well-trained* and very competent people who
haven't got any doctor title (M.D. *or* Ph.D.), but
do have plenty of skill, personality, intelligence, and
compassion. And, psychiatrist or not, *your* super-
shrink might be dressed in faded jeans instead of a
three-piece suit; he might sport long hair or an Afro
instead of a Freud-like little beard. Whoever it is,
the shrink is unwaveringly on your side: he isn't
spying on you, judging you, reforming you, or
merely patting you on the head. He's the creative
listener *you've* hired to help you get to be the
strongest and most honest YOU possible. (That
means you get to accept yourself, clay feet and all.

You don't eliminate all your problems, but you learn better ways of coping with the ones you are stuck with.)

Where does this process take place? Plenty of therapists are in exactly the kind of carpeted offices you've imagined, but some therapists and counselors practice in basements of old churches, or even on park benches where gang members or runaways usually congregate. There are all kinds of agencies and clinics—some where you can just drop in without any appointment and get help without even having to tell your name if you'd rather not.

Now you also know that individual therapy *isn't* the whole story. First, there are group sessions in which several people all work together with a therapist, talking, role-playing, and sharing feelings and insights about each other's problems. Some people like to get that extra feedback which you can't get when it's just you and the therapist; others, however, prefer the privacy and the undivided attention that one-to-one therapy affords. If your parents are game, you can opt for family therapy—which can do wonders for those clogged lines of communication between the generations. There's also a kind of couples counseling which you can get, even if you aren't engaged or married or any particular age.

What if your problem is something very serious: a matter of life or death? Well, you're not out in the cold. Many counselors and therapists are well-equipped to help young women grapple with the feelings—as well as the logistical problems—surrounding an unwanted pregnancy. What if you—or someone you love—are considering suicide? The help you can get is immediate—and lasting. Counseling in this special area is saving lives—every single day.

There is help for runaways, too. A whole network of safe places to stay and get organized, plus sympathetic counseling to help the young person get in touch with what he really wants to do.

Therapy may or may not be for you, but now or sometime in the future, if you do decide to try it, you are way ahead of the game. You know how to find a likely therapist or counselor (neatly avoiding the quacks and clinkers), you know what to expect, you know how to size up your progress. You also know how to deal with potential static from parents, friends, and random snoops.

Sure, a lot of people go into therapy to stop the pain or the anxiety they're suffering, but that doesn't mean it's a crutch or a copout as someone might have told you. In fact, therapy is one very good way of *gaining* control because instead of floating about in a sea of time-wasting, energy-draining dodges and subterfuges, you are finally coming out from under all that helplessness to be in touch, decisive, willing and able to take charge of your own life.

Suggested Further Readings

Here are some thoughtful and fascinating books, full of all sorts of insights.

Cottle, Thomas J. *The Abandoners: Portraits of Loss, Separation, and Neglect.* Boston: Little, Brown & Co., 1972.

Davis, Flora. *Inside Intuition: What We Know About Nonverbal Communication.* New York: McGraw-Hill, 1973.

Glasscote, Raymond M.; Raybin, James B.; Reifler, Clifford B.; and Kane, Andrew W., in collaboration with Feldman, Harvey, and Spivack, Stevan. *The Alternate Services: Their Role in Mental Health. (A Field Study of Free Clinics, Runaway Houses, Counseling Centers and the Like).* Joint Information Service of the American Psychiatric Association and the National Association for Mental Health, 1975.

Gordon, Sol, with Conant, Roger. *YOU: the Psychology of Surviving and Enhancing Your Social Life, Sex Life, School Life, Work Life, Home Life, Emotional Life, Creative Life, Spiritual Life, Style of Life, Life.* New York: A Strawberry Hill Book published with Quadrangle/The New York Times Book Co., 1975.

Konopka, Gisela. *Young Girls: A Portrait of Adolescence.* Englewood Cliffs, N.J.: Prentice-Hall, Inc., 1976.

McGinnis, Dr. Thomas C., and Ayres, John U. *Open Family Living: A New Approach for Enriching Your Life Together.* New York: Doubleday, 1976.

Rosenbaum, Jean. *Is Your Volkswagen a Sex Symbol? What Your Life-style Reveals About You and Your Personality.* New York: Hawthorn Books, 1972.

Shapiro, Evelyn, ed. *Psychosources: A Psychology Resource Catalog.* New York: Bantam/published by arrangement with Communications Research Machines, Inc., 1973.

Index

Abortion, 44, 119, 126, 127, 128-31
Adlerian therapy, 87
Adolescence, 27
Alcoholism, 40, 77, 115, 118
and alcohol counseling centers, 178
Allport, Gordon, 37
American Association of Marriage and Family Counselors, 62-63, 162
American Association of Pastoral Counselors, 48, 63, 162
Anxiety, 26, 31, 43, 78, 85, 86, 184

Baizerman, Michael, 107
Behavior-change therapy, 84-87

Behavior modification therapy. *See* Behavior-change therapy
Bridge Over Troubled Waters, 112-14
Brockman, William, 48, 62

Clergyperson, 38, 47-49, 61, 161, 182
training of, as counselor, 61-62
Counseling, definition of, 61
Counseling Center (Milwaukee), 54, 55, 108-10, 121
Counselors, 26, 61-63. *See also* Couples and marriage counselors; Guidance counselors; Pastoral counselors

187

About the Author

Jane Marks became a professional writer when *Mademoiselle* bought one of her psychology term papers in 1965. Since then, she has written over 100 articles for *Glamour, Town & Country,* and *Seventeen* as well as a variety of other magazines. Though she has covered subjects ranging from experimental education to dieting, ballet, horses, dogs, and ESP, many of her articles are concerned with personal and family problems of young people.

In addition to writing, Ms. Marks is a director and vice president of Windham Child Care, Inc., a voluntary agency in New York, serving teenagers as well as younger children. She is also a collaborator in Social Innovation Information Service, a Washington-based project to promote out-of-classroom learning opportunities for high school students all over the country. Ms. Marks is married to an economist and is the mother of a two-year-old son.